RANCHO PRESS

ARTHUR RIBBEL
Yesterday in San Diego

With illustrations by Virginia Ribbel

RANCHO PRESS: SAN DIEGO

ACKNOWLEDGEMENT

This book is based on columns written for The San Diego Union in the 1980s. The columns have been edited for book publication.

Publishing Consultants, Windsor Associates
Library of Congress catalog card number 90-61926
ISBN 0-9627384-0-9

CONTENTS

YESTERDAY IN SAN DIEGO

ARRIVAL. THE DEPOT

It was a grand trip by train from Nebraska to San Diego in 1915 and it was made even grander by alighting at the new, magnificent San Diego Santa Fe railway station.

The memories of that trip have been refreshed many times by visits to the old Spanish-colonial style depot on Broadway at Kettner Boulevard. It was, indeed, an imposing and elegant edifice then, and it still is, and is included in the National Register of Historic Places. Its domes still glow in the sunlight, the old solid oak benches in the waiting room look sturdy and clean, its striking ceiling rises high and handsome, luggage carts still rattle over spotless and level bricks, and people still hustle to the familiar call of "All aboard!"

But men dressed more formally in 1915 than they do now. They wore suits, felt hats, maybe high shoes, white shirts, ties and possibly a vest with a gold rope chain athwart the chest, one end anchored to an elk's tooth and the other to a thick gold watch. His waist bulge might not have been a paunch, but a money belt.

The ladies didn't appear with bare heads, wearing tank tops, slacks, sandals or tennis shoes, as some do now. Their dresses were long and full, their blouses up to the throat, shoes were high and their hats were weighted down with stacks of feathers, ribbons and bows, berries, flowers and for true elegance possibly a small stuffed bird.

Painted now, and with other renovations to spruce it up, the depot looks a lot like it did in 1915, when it was built to conform to the Spanish architecture of the Panama-California Exposition, a showcase like the train station of this sun-splashed Eden by the sea. By itself, the depot was a hearty and gladsome welcome to the wondering transients from the East and Midwest; by itself, a noble promise of a better life in the sun. Each step, each detail of that day, when a snow-harried prairie family stepped into the San Diego depot, was written large in their diaries and engraved in their memories.

One diary read:

"Left Omaha via Union Pacific for San Diego at 11:55 a.m., Oct. 21, 1916. Snowing.

"Arrived in San Diego via Santa Fe at 6:30 a.m., Oct. 24, and went to the Knickerbocker Hotel. Sunny!"

It was love at first sight between the immigrants and the ornate depot. Everything looked regal, even the restrooms. Its magnificence enhanced the excitement and the lively vibrations within the newcomers. The opulent depot prepared the settlers for the grandeur of the Exposition in Balboa Park.

Although the depot looks much the same now, there is something big missing, a vacancy, an emptiness in the air. Gone are the steam locomotives, the burly and impressive stars of the Age of Steam, those brawny fire-eating iron monsters with the thunderous snorts. Chafing for the gallop, the locomotives bellowed out their blasts and rolled out of the yards headed for the open country.

Small boys, whose sharp eyes caught every detail of the railway and depot, remembered for life the heraldic names on the various cars of the trains. Nor would the lads ever lose from memory the images seen from the train windows: signal lights flashing at night, telegraph poles rushing past, villages, desert, shacks along the right-of-way, a coyote slinking into the brush, seas of corn, cattle, cowboys, people waving, funny little depots, on-rushing scenery, a panorama of America through train car windows, like stereoscopic views seen back home.

For almost 100 years, the railroad station was the main feature of most communities in America. To many town and city people of bygone eras, the railway depot represented the status and wealth of their community, in addition to its cultural and moral standing. Pride, civic esteem, prestige and love went into the building of those old depots. These emotions still have meaning to any San Diegan who takes time to walk to his depot at the foot of Broadway to eye the lofty magnificence of the old place—especially to those who remember and once tingled to the thrill of arrival here.

QUEEN OF BATHHOUSES

The first bit of magnificence an immigrant from the Midwest saw when he swung down from a train at San Diego was the new depot. The second, to the west, was San Diego Bay, blue and bejeweled by the sun, with boats of many dimensions contributing to its charm.

Then, looking to the south across Broadway (earlier named D Street), he saw the impressive entrance to one of the most beautiful natatoriums in the West. Named Los Baños (The Baths), it was the queen of bathhouses in little San Diego 80 years ago, and there are many old-timers who well remember its pleasures and its sounds.

Bathhouse, indeed! It was a spa.

Los Baños was located where the San Diego Gas & Electric Co. powerhouse is today at the foot of Broadway. The newcomer soon learned to call it by its correct name: "Los Ban-yos," instead of the Midwest versions, "Los Bay-nos" or "Los Ban-oss." Through the entrance would come a-roaring the happy shrieks and laughter of boys, girls and adults splashing in the warm salt water which had been pumped from San Diego Bay. It offered a plunge for swimming and fresh-water showers and tub baths for those who had no bathtubs in their homes.

The bay water was clean and pure in the old days and one didn't hesitate to swim in it or to eat fish caught from it. You could see an object on the mud bottom 15 or 20 feet down from your rowboat. In the 1950s, the Navy put the bay out of bounds for swimming because of the pollution.

The electric trolley system made Los Baños possible. A conduit carried bay water to the trolley powerhouse to cool the condensers. As it passed through the power station, the water got hot. Someone had the bright idea of piping this hot water to the bathhouse in order to warm the swimming pool.

It cost 25 cents to use Los Baños. For that you got a bathing suit—long, droopy and gray—a clean towel and a key to one of the small dressing cubicles around the plunge. And if you asked for it, the management would loan you a china doorknob to fling into the tank so you could dive to retrieve it. Patrons could also bring their own bathing suits to avoid the house creations.

A copper-surfaced slide ran down into the water at one side of the tank and the kids shrieked with delight as they shot the chute and piled into the water. Spectators could view the bathers from a space at the entrance end of the bathhouse, and if there were any sneaky-eyed voyeurs among them, they were foiled, for the girls wore voluminous bathing creations which well veiled their charms. The real old-time bathing beauties were capped, shirted, skirted, bloomered, stockinged and slippered. Venus in taffeta!

When the bathhouse palace opened on Aug. 1, 1897, more than 2,000 visitors streamed through it to exclaim with pride and praise over its opulence. Rows of blue-white arc lights, hung from the trusses, illuminated happy throngs that day at Los Baños. Some may have viewed it as another symbol of confidence and optimism for San Diego's future, an optimism that earlier took a dive with the bust of the boom in the 1880s. The opening of the bathhouse was a highlight of the Gay 90s, a decade of little or no growth in which the population of San Diego inched up from 34,987 to a mere 35,090.

Swimmers and just plain soapsuds bathers had a choice of bathhouses stretched along the San Diego Bay waterfront. Rieken's Wharf, on Atlantic Street near Fir Street, was the most northerly of the bathhouses. It was a rickety little wharf with a few dressing rooms and a "pool" which consisted of a corral of wooden fence slabs driven into the mud. In the days before the modern era, San Diego Bay came right up to Atlantic Street, now Pacific Highway.

There were cogent reasons why San Diegans went swimming and bathing at bathhouses. Many had no bathrooms of their own in their homes. The plunges or corrals kept their kids in areas they could supervise. Those who walked on the bottom were protected against the vicious stingarees whose tail barbs caused painful wounds. Dressing rooms and bathing suits could be rented. Some plunges were heated. And it was nice to fraternize over the water.

A legion of youngsters learned to swim at Los Baños. One could come out of Los Baños clean and sweet, walk up town and enjoy a sumptuous meal at Morgan's Cafeteria and then take a trolley to Mission Cliff Gardens and the Ostrich Farm in University Heights for a truly enjoyable day. And so, when the grand plunge closed forever in 1927 to allow for expansion of the gas and electric company's powerhouse, there was nostalgia and sadness at the passing.

THE 1915-1916 EXPO

The buildings were new and marvelous, the landscaping magnificent, and the people of San Diego were enthralled with the Panama-California Exposition of 1915-16.

Grownups being wheeled slowly around the spacious grounds in wicker electric chairs found Balboa Park transformed into a wonderland of structural and botanical beauty, and marveled at the lavish exhibits. The Expo was within 10 minutes of downtown, and Laurel Street ran into the West Gate of the fair.

On the much-heralded opening day, Jan. 1, 1915, President Woodrow Wilson pressed a button 2,600 miles away in Washington, D.C., that turned on a light suspended over the fair by a balloon. It lighted up the fairground for three square miles, the first of many marvels to be seen. The guns of Navy ships in the bay and the cannons nesting at Fort Rosecrans on Point Loma boomed together in a shattering concert as the lights went on.

It was all exciting and dramatic to small wide-eyed boys in short pants, but what they really wanted to know was, "Where's the fun zone called the Isthmus?" They had heard so much about it. Most of the glowing eyewitness accounts of the breathtaking Exposition were written by adults exulting over the buildings, the gardens, the exhibits and the park grounds. The small fry hadn't been heard from in print.

The Isthmus was the old-time pike and midway, the pleasure street, the fun zone of the Expo. It ran north on the east side of the grounds, had a frontage of 8,000 feet and occupied a space of about 25 acres.

San Diego city had a population of only 74,000 then, but folks from far and wide traveled here to view the wonders of San Diego and its fair. Many of them decided to come back and make San Diego their home. The Expo was put on to celebrate the opening of the Panama Canal, but the little Isthmus crawlers paid little heed to that practical matter.

A small menagerie, which boasted of some pacing, growling lions among other beasts, got lots of looking time from the small viewers. It was the beginning of the great San Diego Zoo.

It can be divulged now that some of the more agile boys got in free to the Expo by shinnying up the eucalyptus trees at the west end of Cabrillo Bridge and then swinging Tarzan-like to the wall and over.

They were thrilled to walk hesitatingly through the mysterious dark tunnels of a Chinatown. They strolled the streets of Japan. They listened to the songs of the ukelele, saw the Hawaiian hula dancers in their funny grass skirts, and wondered why so many of the older boys kept hanging around the hula-hulas so long.

There was a diorama of "20,000 Leagues Under the Sea" and one of "The Battle of Manila Bay," complete with sound effects and a realistic shipwreck. There were so many attractions that the boys couldn't decide which to choose and which to put on hold for another day. There was a model of the old San Diego Mission, exhibits of Mexican pottery, a feature entitled "Crossing the Andes," "The Battle of Tijuana," a mountain railway, a Ferris wheel, a roller coaster and a curio bazaar. The crack-crack of a shooting gallery made the boys wish they had more coins in their short pants to spend on the .22-caliber rifles, which were aimed at mechanical ducks moving in water. You could buy wonderful ice cream, soda water and candy on the Isthmus.

The children's parents didn't have to worry about them being run over in traffic at the Expo. The only vehicle permitted on the grounds was the small wicker motor chair known as an "Electriquette," which carried two or three persons and was limited to 3 miles per hour. They were called "joy cars" but any attempts at joy-riding in them were frowned upon.

Almost everybody who attended the Expo said it was like "gilding the lily to have such a marvelous show in San Diego's marvelous climate and marvelous setting, and with its marvelous bay and marvelous people."

Some big men saw the fair, like William Jennings Bryan, William Howard Taft, "Uncle Joe" Cannon, the speaker of the House of Representatives, Franklin D. Roosevelt, then assistant secretary of the Navy, Thomas Edison and former President Theodore Roosevelt. The small boys wondered if they took in the Isthmus.

The Liberty Bell, which all boys and girls had heard about in school, came to the Expo for three days, then returned to its home in Philadelphia.

The fair went on through 1916, with new amusements and new exhibits. Then it closed. The beloved Isthmus was torn down, except for the Indian village and the animal cages. Young and old remember the famed opera star, Madame Ernestine Schumann-Heink, singing "Auld Lang Syne" on the Organ Pavilion stage with tears in her eyes as the Expo closed. Fireworks spelled out the message, "World's Peace, 1917." Within four months, the United States had declared war on Germany—and the fair was over.

HATFIELD

In years when rain has been scarce and calls go out for water conservation, the memories of many older San Diegans go back to Hatfield the Rainmaker. And by this time, Charley Mallory Hatfield has become a folk figure throughout America.

It was in December 1915, and the rain runoff into the reservoirs of San Diego had been below normal, when the City Council got a letter from the rainmaker which read:

"I will fill the Morena Reservoir to overflowing between now and Dec. 20, 1916, for the sum of $10,000, in default of which I ask no compensation, or I will deliver at the Morena Reservoir 30 inches of rain free of charge, you to pay the $500 per inch from the 30th to the 50th inch, all above 50 inches to be free, on or before the first of June 1916."

The council voted to accept Hatfield's offer to fill Morena Reservoir and City Atty. T. B. Cosgrove was directed to draw up a contract. But the contract was never signed.

Hatfield confidently moved his equipment by wagon to Morena Lake and began his rainmaking. He never disclosed the chemicals he used. Clouds rolled in and a steady rain began to fall on Jan. 14. Was it Hatfield or an act of God? The city attorney advised that no money should be paid until Hatfield proved that he was making the rain fall in quantity.

The rain became a downpour. The San Diego River rose. People flocked to the old Mission Cliff Gardens to view the phenomenon of the river raging angrily through Mission Valley. Bridges were washed out. One resident of the flooded valley, rescued by rowboat, wiped the rain from his brow and exclaimed, "Let's pay Hatfield $100,000 to quit!"

A part of Sweetwater Dam washed away, as did Lower Otay. And it kept on raining.

The rampaging San Diego River swept away houses and barns. Cattle drowned and crops were destroyed, boats were swept from their moorings, the coast road to Los Angeles was impassable, and some telephone communications went out. Streams ran through Balboa Park, and there was fear the deluge would ruin the Expo buildings. Cows, horses, mules, sheep and goats were driven from their pens and corrals and wandered about the streets. There were wild rumors that irate farmers were looking for Hatfield.

At long last, the rains abated. Damages ran into the millions, and Hatfield's claim for pay for services rendered was rejected by the City Council. Hatfield sued, but on advice of the city attorney, the city contested the suit. Hatfield offered to reduce his claim to $4,000, but that, too, was rejected. Later, a court dismissed Hatfield's suit.

Shelley Higgins, then assistant city attorney, said he told Hatfield's lawyer the city would pay the claim if he agreed to accept responsibility for the flood damage. Higgins said Hatfield's attorney "told us to go to hell."

At least, soggy San Diegans would have been able to get dry there.

ARMISTICE

At the eleventh hour of the eleventh day of the eleventh month, on the morning of Nov. 11, 1918, the Armistice was signed in a railway car in the small French town of Compiègne to end bloody World War I, the war to end all wars.

The exciting news flashed around the world and little San Diego burst into jubilation. Who among those who were there can ever forget that Armistice Day, and night, in downtown San Diego?

Mayor Louis J. Wilde issued a proclamation:

"We are closing the most perfect day in all history with trumpets, shouts of gladness and charitable thanksgiving."

The City Council declared a half-holiday, stores closed and the Chamber of Commerce made hasty plans for an afternoon parade with the cooperation of military authorities. Camp Kearny was under quarantine because of the terrible influenza epidemic which had killed thousands throughout the world, but infantrymen wearing gauze masks arrived in time to participate.

The site for Camp Kearny had been leased on Linda Vista Mesa. The camp was named after Gen. Stephen Watts Kearny, who had led an expeditionary force into California in the war with Mexico in 1846. A mounted force of Californios, armed with long lances, gave Kearny's troopers a bad mauling at the Battle of San Pasqual in San Diego County in 1846.

The masked soldiers from the camp formed ranks with sailors and Marines at the foot of Broadway and moved to Horton Plaza, the heart and the ground for so many of the city's patriotic celebrations and rallies.

Most people walked the streets in masses laughing and calling to each other, seemingly eager to celebrate but not knowing exactly how to do it. Autos dashed madly up and down the streets, some of them dragging cowbells and tin cans.

A sea of white sailor hats moved with the tide of human waves. Girls were hugged by men. One 14-year-old boy spectator at Fourth and Broadway reported to his peers in short pants the next day, with some disgust and disapproval, that "some of the grown-ups were huggin' and kissin'." To him, the mighty roar of the crowd downtown was awesome. He never forgot it.

Celebrants in hotel windows above the crowds showered the people below with talcum powder rather than confetti. Confetti was in short supply.

There had been meatless days, much knitting of scarves and socks for soldiers, and spontaneous fund-raising for the Red Cross and patriotic groups. On poles and in windows, war posters still stared out: "Can vegetables and fruit, and the Kaiser too!" "Uncle Sam wants you!" "You can help win the war!" "The Navy needs you!" "Remember Belgium!"

Overheard at the Plaza was this question, "Now that the war is over, what will they find to put in the newspapers?" With no radios then to broadcast the news, the folks in the residential districts learned of the war's end from newsboys running through the neighborhood yelling, "Extra, extra, war is over!"

Patriotism during the war had taken some bizarre turns. Hamburger was renamed Liberty Steak; sauerkraut, Liberty Cabbage. People with German names were called by phone and threatened and insulted. A boy named Kaiser was shot in the behind with a BB gun.

The war wrought such changes as more women wearing silk stockings, shorter skirts and even make-up. Men were introduced to wristwatches, which were worn in the trenches. The war raised America's standard of living, bolstered the strength of labor unions, increased cigarette smoking by both men and women, and loosened the nation's morals, among other changes.

The naive doughboys who went to the muddy hell of the trenches Over There came back with eyes opened, never to be quite so trusting again.

THE FLU

The Germans were licked. The truce was on. San Diego looked forward to peace and prosperity and a bountiful Thanksgiving.

But another foe, more sinister than armies, remained to be conquered in 1918-19—the Spanish influenza.

It seems unreal, looking back. Joyous people were celebrating the armistice while wearing masks to ward off the flu, an implacable killer. Before its three waves subsided, it had infected a billion people and killed 20 million. The Black Death of 1347-1350 killed 60 million, but the flu was the biggest plague of modern times.

Eleven cases broke out at Camp Kearny here in late September 1918. Within a month, there were 329 cases in the city, and 11 deaths in one day. During all of 1918, there were more than 4,000 cases and 324 deaths in the city. That was the worst of it. In 1919, there were about 650 cases and 44 deaths.

In the country as a whole, more than half a million people died, more than the number of Americans who died in Europe in the war. Throughout the country, schools, theaters and other public places were closed under a general quarantine. All stores in San Diego were closed for three days in early December, when a new wave of flu cases was reported here. The city schools finally reopened in January 1919.

San Diego enacted a health requirement. Citizens, young and old, must wear a gauze mask as a protective measure. Pads of gauze fastened over the mouth and nose by strings tied behind the head were prescribed. It was believed that the masks kept out the flu germs just as screens kept flies off front porches. But some critics said the masks were not impervious enough to do the job.

Small boys and girls played marbles while peering over their gauze and complained the masks interfered with their shooting and their baseball playing. The masks were stowed away in their pockets when their parents and teachers weren't looking.

Health officials complained some adults also took the masks too lightly. Some men cut holes in them so they could smoke cigars. Citizens had to remove their masks in crowded restaurants to eat. Those who didn't wear masks were called "slackers" and were shunned in some quarters.

Some political Californians protested that the mask edict amounted to unconstitutional interference with personal liberty. But placards urging, "Wear a mask and save your life!" were posted throughout the state. And Gov. William D. Stephens proclaimed Gauze Mask Use Day.

We were told to be effective the masks must be worn at all times when people were together, must be washed and dried daily, and must be of proper thickness. Goggles also were recommended. Women were warned against walking outside barefooted or in flimsy slippers.

Some masks were designed with an extended snout, like Miss Piggy's. Some women styled their masks with harem-like veils hanging loose below the chin.

The disease was called Spanish because it was believed to have started in the town of San Sebastian, Spain. From there it spread like wildfire. It invaded American armed forces en route to Europe. Navy men had a high rate of infection. President Woodrow Wilson caught the flu while at the Paris peace conference and it left him weak.

The epidemic ended as mysteriously as it began, leaving people worried and wondering if it would ever strike again. But people forget. H. L. Mencken, the sage of Baltimore, commenting in 1956 on the great epidemic of 1918-19, wrote:

"The epidemic is seldom mentioned, and most Americans have apparently forgotten it. This is not surprising. The human mind always tries to expunge the intolerable from memory, just as it tries to conceal it while current."

HILLCREST

The residents of Hillcrest in earlier days seemed quietly satisfied that their community was a first-rate place in which to live.

The neighborhood was calm, sufficient, handy, compact, well-ventilated by breezes, verdant and neighborly—so went the happy conclusions. It was a village within the city of San Diego. The boundaries were never defined to the satisfaction of many people—Washington Street on the north, Park Boulevard to the east, Walnut or Upas streets to the south, and some canyons and streets to the west.

It was a bedroom community, although as the years jogged on, businesses intruded into some of the residential headlands. The Manifest Destiny of downtown was up the hills to the mesas, and Hillcrest was one terminus of that migration. Fifth Street—it was street then, not avenue—led to Hillcrest and to what was called Pill Hill because of the number of doctors', dentists' and laboratory offices on its slopes.

The heart of Hillcrest was, and is, Fifth and University avenues. You could board a No. 3 or No. 1 street car downtown for the three-mile journey to the heart of Hillcrest. A boy on a bicycle would coast downtown on Fifth in a jiffy. Coming back was tougher.

Hillcresters liked to believe that Mission Valley was part of their village. They looked down then on a different valley than they do today, a garden land of small farms and dairies, rather than giant shopping centers, office buildings, hotels, motels, sprawling condominium developments, restaurants, service stations and a golf course.

North and northwest of Hillcrest was the area called Mission Hills, which rated itself as more elite than Hillcrest.

Modest, single-family homes clustered in Hillcrest, occupied by many former residents of the Corn Belt states, the Snowbirds who came here to escape the freezing winter snow and sleet of the Midwest and East. They had a new, different and more comfortable lifestyle in sunny San Diego, or Sun Diego.

The annual state picnics held in nearby Balboa Park were big events in those days. They were marked by bulging hampers of delicious food which was prepared by housewife gourmets.

The planners of Hillcrest were generous in their allotment of space. Homes had spacious front and back yards and alleys ran behind many for deliveries and garbage and rubbish cans. Some folks kept chickens for both eggs and meat in their back yards beneath their fruit trees, and they went to Irwin's Hay and Grain store at 10th and University to buy feed.

Old Hillcrest, indeed, was a microcosm of a small town. There were doctors, a dentist, a theater, its own newspaper, a drugstore, groceries, barbershops. There was a school, post office, two hospitals, a fire department, a bike shop, bank and many other ingredients of a village with the area well-serviced by street cars.

There is fond remembrance of the hell-raising and spine-tingling serials which livened Saturday afternoons at the Hillcrest Theater at 3825 Fifth St.—such shows as "Madagascar Madness," "Mystery Ship," and "The Perils of Pauline."

E. O. Oliver was the proprietor of a bicycle shop at 512 University Ave. To the boys, Oliver's was more, much more than just a bike shop. A man with gnarled hands and kindly face, Oliver presided over displays of shiny, exciting new bikes in the front and a homey repair shop in the rear, where the small fry gathered around and watched Mr. Oliver work marvels in curing their ailing bikes. At the same time, he would be propounding gems of wisdom for the lads.

The school was Florence Grammar School at First and University, where boys in short pants, caps, high shoes and blouse-like shirts, and girls with starched dresses and hair tied with ribbons, would line up in front of the school each morning and then march to their respective classes to the accompaniment of a march played by a pupil on the piano.

All things considered, the old-time folks remember the Hillcrest cavalcade with a smile.

SCHOOL DAYS

Boys and girls trudging to Florence Grammar School in Hillcrest each morning so many years ago had a different experience from today's youngsters.

Elementary schools were called grammar schools then and, remembering the diagrammed sentences and memorized parts of speech, they seem to have been well named.

First off, all children walked to the venerable red brick schoolhouse at First and University, no parents drove them, no buses picked them up. It was not expected that they would walk in a straight line to the schoolhouse, but would, like kids of all generations, take many detours, zig-zags and ups and downs before ending their journey. Instead of using the walkway over a bridge spanning a canyon, they would climb down into the canyon and up the other side, taking with them to class the aroma of sage and other bushes of the chaparral, plus a few burrs on stockings.

On their laggard, but unforgettable journeys, they might have heard the quail crying, "Beware, beware," have seen cottontail rabbits vanish in the thick brush, viewed horned toads disappearing into their hiding places, followed a butterfly and found a bluejay's feather.

They carried with them, in plain brown grocery bags, sandwiches of peanut butter, pimiento cheese, jelly, olive spread, canned ham or leftover chicken. Sometimes they ate part of their lunch on the way to school. Some of them left their pet dogs on their home doorsteps, watching mournfully while their masters went off.

Very few objects, scenes or actions were missed by the sharp eyes of boys and girls on their walks to school. A child's eyes see so much more. The skies seemed clearer then, the air fresher—and maybe they were.

Traffic was much lighter on the streets then, and there were no crossing guards in orange jackets, herding the kids across the intersections near school, and no flashing traffic signals. The word "segregation" wasn't in the vocabulary of these youngsters; they took the newcomers as they came and didn't pose any questions or doubts. There weren't any drug problems, unless boys trying to smoke corn silk or the medicinal cigarettes called "cubebs" could be called using drugs, which it was not.

School was a safe haven, unless you hadn't done your homework. Of course, every school had a few bums and bullies who set a pace of wrongdoing, like smoking cigarettes after school behind fences, and picking on smaller boys.

Crime was low, but there were boys on the way to school who cased some loquat, orange, apricot or guava trees in the backyards of householders for future pilfering. Backyards were interesting anyway. There might be coops of egg-laying chickens, rabbits raised for meat, or a goat or two for milk.

The boys wore high shoes, possibly with buttons, black cotton stockings, corduroy knee pants, broadcloth shirts and string ties, topped off with a cap. The boys sympathized with the girls for having no pockets in their dresses to carry such important treasures as a rabbit's foot for good luck, a small paper-wad shooter for instant retaliation in case of a sudden attack in the classroom, a candy jawbreaker and a piece of licorice whip. Also there might be an all-purpose jackknife, a length of fishing string, rattlesnake rattles, a bit of wood bark and an assortment of marbles of all values—dobies, glassies, steelies and agates.

For those youngsters who graduated from grammar school in those days, there was the big jump to San Diego High across town. Grade schools taught all eight grades—there were no junior high schools—and the difference between a lofty eighth-grader and a lowly high school freshman was a big one.

The old red brick Florence schoolhouse is no longer. It was torn down in 1961 after serving faithfully for 53 years and turning out legions of youngsters. But not torn down were the rich memories of thousands of children who had tramped its halls and marched smartly up the front steps to the tune of an old piano and the beat of a triangle.

YESTERDAY'S GIRLS

Every now and then, in the days just before the 1920s, a love-smitten boy would carry to school the books of his one and only. And in so doing, he often elicited the jeers, catcalls and taunts of his boy peers, who may have been jealous.

"I sure wish I was a boy," was a line heard about 70 years ago from a girl who envied the freedom of her brothers. Girls had no pockets, those wonderful repositories of boyhood treasures. They didn't have copper toes on their shoes, as boys' shoes did. Their parents thought the ladylike games they were supposed to engage in wouldn't wear out the toes the way the boys' activities did.

But girls had pretty colored ribbons in their hair, fresh, crisp dresses that complemented their pretty faces, long curls or maybe pigtails, high shoes and long cotton stockings. No jeans and no tank tops.

The boys might wonder what the girls did with themselves all day when they weren't allowed to go hunting, fishing or hiking alone; they couldn't play football or wrestle or read *Captain Billy's Whiz Bang,* a racy periodical of the age. Girls never would try chewing tobacco, go trapping, shoot guns or go skinny dipping in a wild pond. They couldn't build things with erector sets, shoot marbles on the school grounds or crawl into a cave alone.

At recess at grammar school, the girls had to play on one side of the playground and the boys on the other. No mingling. When a class baseball team was organized, it was composed solely of boys. The same for the school football and basketball teams.

There were Maypole dances on the playground, and the girls predominated there, but to the boys' everlasting embarrassment and secret enjoyment, some of them were required to partner the girls as they danced.

The teachers, all women, wore conservative long, dark skirts and white or pastel blouses, and the principal had on a most conservative dark suit to go with his dignified stance and white shirt and tie.

The girl who got to beat the triangle during the march into school each morning probably was the teacher's pet. Few boys aspired to be teacher's pets.

There was no uniformity of style in the girls' hair ribbons. They were all sorts: big bunches, long streamers, butterfly bows. Everyone's personality was expressed in ribbon.

For the girls there were no polyester dresses, but nice cotton, starched, hard-to-iron ones, some with even harder-to-iron ruffles. All girls wore stockings at all times, some with high shoes and some with low shoes.

What did the younger girls do in those days? They played with dolls. Girls played jacks with a ball and jacks. They played ball and swam with their brothers. They went to dancing schools and dances. They went to movies, peered into stereoscopes and listened to the Victrola. They had giggly pajama parties. They played musical instruments and took piano lessons. They went to summer camps after the camps were carefully surveyed by their parents. They could go boating, with proper company. They could play "Post Office," the mild kissing game, if they were properly policed by responsible parents. They changed slowly, oh so slowly, from the tight restrictions of Victorian days.

Much of their activity related to making a home, emulating Mother in her ceaseless work around the house—washing clothes, doing the dishes, cooking, ironing, scrubbing, caring for younger children, dusting and many other tasks designed to develop girls into housewives.

The tomboys among the girls seemed to know no season and recognized only the taboos they chose to honor. But they were the exception.

Most girls were giggles, kisses on the cheek, blushes, smiles, a hop, skip and a jump, a whispered secret, a passing fear and a passing tear. A romp, a wave of the hand, a ribbon and a Valentine, a doll, a bow, an ardent face, carefree thoughts and so many other warm and tender features.

Yesterday's girls hoarded their good memories for the sterner decades ahead.

BALBOA PARK

The many little things blending with the big attractions went toward making San Diego's Balboa Park a world-famous garden land and playground.

The little things might have been missed by big people but caught the eyes of youngsters. Quail could be seen running beneath the shrubbery off Sixth Avenue near Upas Street, and then ascending in a whirring covey. Rabbits scurried for cover in the brush in the canyons.

The expanses of lawn off Sixth Avenue furnished football fields and baseball diamonds for boys and girls. At one stretch, there were natural goal posts at each end—trees side by side.

Mothers did not worry then for the safety of their daughters exploring the acres of the park. Crimes didn't occur so often as they do now. These remarks apply to the teens and the 20s, when San Diego was still young and the respect and appreciation of the people were high.

Looking back, the entire park was clean and relatively unused. Even the grass was strong and green and untrampled.

Climbing the California Tower was a challenge to youngsters puffing up the long stairs. The view from the tower for them was unforgettable.

The flowers, trees, shrubs, wildlife and spectacular buildings combined to create magic scenes for kids looking skyward.

A day in the park for a child with a brown-bag lunch and a bottle of pop was sufficient in those good green years for most of the youngsters. It was even a thrill to look over the railings of Cabrillo Bridge and see the lily pond far below, reflecting the sun.

Not so many airplanes roared overhead then to disrupt the communing of the people with their beautiful park and its lovely scenes, like the botanical gardens or the Plaza de Panama.

The great Organ Pavilion, of course, has not been rated as a lesser attraction for the kids. Many of them sat composed and entertained at the organ concerts of J. Humphrey Stewart, the talented organist of many years ago. Some of the kids later marched at the pavilion as high school graduates.

The city trustees of the last century, who dedicated the park, may have never fully envisioned the riches their "City Park" (later renamed Balboa Park) would provide for future generations—or the cruel desecrations committed against the park by unthinking and unappreciative people.

When the transplanted people from all over the globe wrote to their former neighbors down home, Balboa Park was prominent in their praise of this paradise by the southern sea.

KATE SESSIONS

No chronicle of the eminent women of San Diego can be complete without the story of Kate Olivia Sessions, horticulturist, nursery owner and beautifier of the earth, 1857-1940.

Her popular title, "Mother of Balboa Park," tells something of her worth to San Diego, but the full story of the tributes and honors she received would take many pages to tell. Trees and flowers in Balboa Park and the gratitude of many San Diegans are memorials to her talents, her generosity and her accomplishments.

We remember Kate in her garden attire: the inevitable hat, the long flowered house dress, sensible shoes and perhaps a light sweater. There might have been a little garden dirt on the hem of her dress.

The trees she planted in the park were many and majestic. Boys and girls gazed in wonder at Katie's cork trees in the park. She was fond of young children.

She helped many beautify and develop their yards and gardens, and for that San Diegans were forever grateful.

She was born in San Francisco and graduated from the University of California at Berkeley in 1881 with a bachelor of science degree. She was one of the best-looking co-eds at the university. Surprisingly at that time when women scientists were few, she studied botany, horticulture and agriculture.

When the Russ School was opened in San Diego in 1882, she was hired as one of the first faculty members, fresh out of college. Russ School was later renamed Russ High School and then became San Diego High School. In 1887, she decided to take up a career in horticulture and quit teaching. Coronado was being developed. Kate went there to open a nursery, and she started a cut-flower depot in San Diego. She grew many new varieties of plants and trees and many notables visited her Coronado nursery.

On Feb. 17, 1892, the City Council passed an ordinance granting the young woman "the right to use and occupy certain lands of the City Park (later named Balboa Park)." She was to establish an experimental nursery and garden for the development of the park for a period not exceeding 10 years, with water privileges. The agreement provided that she would annually plant and care for 100 varied sorts of trees for the use of the city. In addition, she was to furnish the city 300 ornamental trees in crocks or boxes.

Her lease was at the northwest corner of the park, at Sixth and Upas and covered about 30 acres. Her flower fields extended down the canyon to what is now the Cabrillo Freeway (Highway 163). She moved her nursery business from Coronado and leased the spacious Crittenden House, on Upas between 6th and 7th, as a home.

The planting at City Park was not all easy. Kate had to blast holes in the cement-like hardpan and move rocks to make holes large enough to plant trees. During one period, she had to haul barrels of water in horse-drawn carts. One of her prize plantings was a tipu tree which stood in the park for years.

Wherever she went she created beauty. She was especially successful with chrysanthemums and carnations. Carnations became the city of San Diego's official flower. She had a flower shop in downtown San Diego and decided Horton Plaza looked bare. So in 1897, she planted 28 young *Cocos plumosa* palms there.

She moved her nursery to the corner of Stephens and Lark streets in Mission Hills and helped her brother, Frank, get started in the business of raising poinsettias.

About 1914, she and Frank moved their operations to Pacific Beach, where they acquired 67 acres at the foot of Mount Soledad. A park near her nursery site now bears her name, as does the nearby Kate Sessions

Elementary School.

San Diego's beloved Kate Sessions died at the age of 83 on Easter Sunday, March 24, 1940. Her mourners remembered the Easter flowers she had furnished for San Diegans for many years and the Bradley-Woolman Mortuary Chapel was almost filled with flowers at her funeral. Civic leaders, including George W. Marston, served as honorary pallbearers. She was buried under a mound of flowers in Mount Hope Cemetery beside her father, mother and brother.

BYGONE MISSION VALLEY

How the sounds and scenery in old Mission Valley have changed!

The roar of freeway traffic, planes, commerce and industry have taken the place of bird songs and the lowing of cattle. The contrast seems unbelievable to old-timers.

They saw a garden of small farms and dairies, not the business and industry visible today. It was a tranquil and beautiful checkerboard of well-manicured truck farms, planted in alfalfa, corn, cabbage, beans, squash and other green produce. They saw peaceful dairies and the San Diego River bubbling up here and there from its upside-down position beneath the sand;

in summer, a green isle in memory.

The valley, from its Spanish beginnings to the shopping center development after the 1950s, was home to polo playing, farming, dairy and hog farming, fishing in potholes, hunting, hiking, horseback riding, beekeeping and sheepherding. Many oldsters recall hunting rabbits, quail and dove on the floor of the valley.

Boys of the past remember hiking to the valley down Sixth Street or threading their way through thick brush below the county hospital (now University Hospital), generally at the end of Front and First streets, with gun, lunch and canteen. Then a boy looked down upon a fresh and lush panorama, akin to a Grant Wood painting. A lowing of cows, the neighing of horses, and the reveille of roosters ushered in the early morn; meadowlarks sang their matin melodies; there were other sounds of the farms and dairies awakening for the day—the clump-clump of field horses and, maybe, an occasional chug-chug of a Model T Ford. No freeways then cut the pastoral scenes of green and gold, and rich black bottom land. But those days are gone, never to return.

The valley has long been marked as a path of history. In 1769, when the padres established the mission and San Diego began in Old Town and on Presidio Hill, they had to walk to the river and sink buckets into sandy water holes for fresh water. On the banks of the San Diego, the first bells rang out in California. The first mules, horses and cattle were seen. The Padres' Dam on the river was the first irrigation project built on the Pacific Coast.

San Diegans looking down from a valley rim not so long ago saw no flood control works, no great shining edifices, little paving, no stadium, no freeways. Downtown San Diego, four or five miles away, seemed distant. Shooting stars, pinks, lupines, violets, poppies and asters adorned the slopes and flats. Windmills spun busily, horses whinnied in the morning stillness, and harvest sounds enriched the pastoral air. Rim-dwellers exulted in the loveliness below, and all seemed to be at peace with the world.

GROCERY STORES

Those newcomers who settled in San Diego between 1910 and 1920 found the city dotted with homey little grocery stores. They were a helpful part of many neighborhoods, and filled a need until chain stores and supermarkets drove them out.

There are still small grocery stores throughout the city and county, but they are apt to be called "convenience stores." In older days, they were called the grocery store or the corner store, and they were entirely different from today's convenience stores. They had names, often that of the owner, or something like Golden Rule Grocery, which wasn't a bad name at all for a store.

People really dressed up to go shopping downtown, but they felt comfortable in their "seconds" at the corner grocery, where the manager often was covered with a long white apron worn over wide suspenders.

A big difference between shopping in the old grocery stores and shopping today is that the owner or clerk would get each item of your order for you, be it on high shelves or in baskets out front or inside. He might deftly pick a box off a high shelf with a pair of tongs at the end of a long pole, or he might climb a high ladder behind the counter which slid along the shelves. As you ordered the next thing on your list, he might go across the store or in back to get it and bring it back to the counter.

Courtesy and friendliness were two of the products Mr. Grocery Man offered free of charge and in large quantities. He dealt with neighbors, and he treated them with consideration and kindness. He was regarded by his customers as a benefactor.

"Good morning, Mrs. Casey, and how are you this morning?" might be the greeting one summer day for Mrs. Casey as she entered the screen door. A bell attached to the door announced the arrival of a customer.

The stores had either a cash register or a cash drawer with compartments for bills and coins. The storekeeper kept rows of note pads in slots in a box, on which he tallied the purchases and their prices and the date. At the end of the month he would add up the orders and present the customer with the monthly bill. Often he would add some fruit or a bag of candy to the order on the day the patron paid up his bill promptly.

The defaulters, somehow or other, were marked people around the neighborhood, and they were not classed as No. 1 citizens or neighbors. They were branded in the neighborhood gossip circles as dead-beats. If the debtor went too deeply into debt at the store, his pad was removed from the credit box, and he was served on a cash-only basis, which was shameful and disgraceful, in the estimation of the neighborhood.

Some of the neighborhood groceries delivered and you could call in your order in the morning and it was delivered that afternoon. The owner-manager of a little neighborhood store answered the phone himself, of course, and took the orders. If he had a delivery man, he would be sent to the back door of the homes and would deliver the order to the lady of the house.

Sometimes the better boys of the neighborhood would dutifully haul the family's groceries home in their coaster wagons. Really enterprising boys might linger outside with their wagons hoping to be hired by someone with a large grocery order and thereby to earn a nickel or a dime—big money in those days.

Some of the new folks in town wouldn't buy a house unless it had a small grocery store handy, that is, within walking distance.

In most of the small neighborhood stores, bushel baskets, both outside and inside, carried bulk food, including beans, peas, fruit, potatoes and other vegetables and grains. Cookies and crackers were also sold unpackaged in bulk. Cheese came in big rounds. Small boys never failed to become fascinated at the cheese cutter in his wielding of the big knife. The grocer always offered a small tasting piece of the cheeses to the customer before the final choice was made.

A store's counter was crowded with candy-stick jars, a roll of heavy wrapping paper, scales, a coffee grinder and the cash box. String hung down from a huge ball enclosed in a wrought-iron holder. There wasn't any tape in those days and all packages were tied. The old-type scales, with a tinny basket on chains, rattled merrily in the old stores as the grocer weighed out sugar or flour and poured it into brown bags.

Vinegar was kept in a 5-gallon jug and was poured out in small bottles. Kerosene was poured from a barrel at the rear of the store into gallon cans brought by customers.

The candy counters were the domain of the small fry: caramel chews, licorice whips, all-day suckers which lasted only about a half hour, jawbreakers, chocolates, fudge, cherry flips, cluster ruffs, lemon drops, red-hots, marshmallows, chewing gum and horehound candy. Sarsaparilla drink came in bottles, and a wonderful taste it had, too.

The aromas, ah, the fragrances of the little old grocery stores stick in the memory. There was the scent of coffee being ground, spices, fruit, pickles in a barrel, cheese, cookies, crackers, apples, peaches, candy and many other good smells. And don't forget the sauerkraut!

Looking back, those little stores were more than neighborhood groceries. They were institutions.

PEDDLERS

The aproned housewife of yesterday, working in a simpler age, opened her doors in the course of her day to an array of peddlers heralded by different sounds and cries. She understood the different horns, bells, whistles and shouts, and responded accordingly, often buying products or services from different vehicles parked at her curb.

The mail man always blew a whistle after he had dropped the letters through the slot in the front door or into a box affixed to a front porch post or pillar.

"Mail man!" he would shout.

A rustle and banging from the service porch was followed by the familiar call of "Ice man!"—a reassuring sound. If her ice company card was tilted to the number 25 in a front window, the man knew she wanted a 25-pound chunk delivered to her icebox; if a larger chunk was needed, the card would be turned to that number. Meanwhile, the kids, like ice locusts, would clean his ice wagon of the cold, dripping chips.

The scissors sharpener blew on a distinctive whistle to notify the ladies of the neighborhood that he was standing by to sharpen scissors and knives. He used a mobile contraption containing grinding wheels and tools, and he powered it by foot.

"Any rags, bottles or sacks?" was the cry of the junkman, driving either a one-horse wagon or a beat-up old truck to carry off metals, cast-off utensils, tools, paper and other household jetsam, which he was prepared to purchase.

Impudent gamins, standing on the curb, would shout, "What did you eat for dinner?"

Back would come the answer, "Rags, bottles, sacks!"

The tinkle of the milkman's bottles and cans in the early mornings was another familiar and reassuring sound. The cream was all at the top of a bottle then, and some people poured a little off to use with coffee. At first, a horse pulled the milk cart and stood patiently by the curb at the homes of customers while the milkman delivered his bottles and picked up notes for more orders. He also picked up a bottle with money inside it to pay for previous deliveries. His horse moved forward to meet him after his deliveries when it heard his piercing whistle.

There was a picturesque little fish peddler's horse cart, with a box-like body carrying a variety of fish on ice. It also carried scales, an assortment of knives, towels, wrapping paper and a large horn which gave out a honk akin to a foghorn blast. With that horn, there was no doubt that he had moored his little wagon to the curb and was awaiting the housewives to come to him and select their fresh fish—halibut, sea bass, rock cod, smelt, flounder, perch and other species caught in local waters.

The operator of that mobile little fish market was an engaging little chunk of an Italian, wearing old trousers, cap, apron, leather wrist-protectors and a knife.

First he would blow the horn and then he would shout, "Fresha feesh!" Then he would drop the counter at the rear of his tiny cart.

There was a Chinese vegetable peddler who drove a rickety old truck. It made so much noise that he didn't have to announce his arrival by horn, whistle or bell.

Many meat markets delivered then. Charles Hardy, at one time the town's leading meat dealer, operated mobile butcher-shop trucks. The butcher cut the desired roast or chops at the curb in front of your house.

The bakery man, too, delivered to residential streets, opening his rear door to a mouth-watering assortment of cakes, pies, muffins, bread and other goodies.

There were other visitors. From around corners, fascinated boys and girls would stare at colorfully clothed Gypsies coming to the front door, wanting to tell fortunes for cash.

And hobos were in the gallery of characters who

came to the door of our housewife. They loved San Diego's warm weather in winter. Some filtered through the cordon of police, constables and railroad detectives and made their way to homes to beg for food, clothing and money.

The housewife of yesterday did, indeed, open her door to a fascinating world of characters, always with the good humor of simpler times.

THE SUNDAY DRIVE

The good old Sunday drive. Is the custom still with us, or has it been smothered by clogged highways and violent, fearsome freeways? It was a part of Americana between 1910 and 1920, with a bit of edging into the 1920s and 30s.

Driving to the beach, to the mountains, taking Grandma out for a spin in the fresh air, wheeling beyond the city limits to buy fresh vegetables, fruit and eggs, or just going for a drive to nowhere for the fun of it. Whatever the reason, it was the thing to do after church and Sunday dinner.

The big traditional Sunday dinner had been eaten; Sunday church and Sunday School had been religiously attended. The open road beckoned to Mr. and Mrs. California and all the little Californians in their big, open touring car with the top down. The Sunday drive took the place of the Sunday nap or the Sunday stroll.

Unless you were going to rough it at a picnic in the wilds, the mores of the day dictated that you wear your Sunday clothes for the drive. But car trouble could be rough going. In 1916, the equipment recommended for a jaunt in the car included:

Rubber lap robes, goggles, a tow rope, pump, tire-patching kit, reserve cans of gasoline and oil, a compass, spotlight, chains, a 2-inch wooden plank to support the jack, and canvas water bags for man and car, among other necessities, such as a shovel. There were relatively few paved roads.

Room always could be found for the big picnic hamper carrying a gourmet treasure, which included cold beef left over from Sunday dinner, pickled eggs, bread and butter or rolls, pickles, watermelon, fried chicken, potato salad, pie, milk, iced sarsaparilla and stomach powders. Some folks got carsick.

The motorist didn't have to go far, though, to find a truck farm, fruit orchard or chicken ranch in Mission Valley, Chollas Heights, the San Luis Rey Valley, Spring Valley, Poway, Lemon Grove, Chula Vista, La Mesa, Vista, Otay and many other familiar places.

The car was kept safe in the garage all week. Washing and polishing it every Saturday was routine. It was taken out and driven only on Sundays.

This led to the canard that the Sunday driver was ultraconservative and so cautious that he constituted a road hazard. "You drive like a Sunday driver" was an epithet even then.

Many a new car changed the lifestyle of citizens from New York to San Diego between 1900 and 1916. At the turn of the century there were 21 million horses in the U.S. and only 4,000 automobiles. By 1916, there were more than 3 million cars and the number of horses had declined precipitately.

So you think the roads of today are crowded? In March of 1918, the entire seven states west of the Rockies had one car for every 10 people in California. "If the roads seem crowded," explained one travel writer of the day, "that's why."

OCEAN BEACH BRIDGE

In 1915 a railway company built a 1,500-foot long, 50-foot wide wooden bridge over the mouth of Mission Bay between Ocean Beach and Mission Beach. That was the dull, factual notation of the birth of the old Ocean Beach bridge.

It didn't in any manner even hint at the future the bridge had in the lives of small boys in short pants and high shoes about 65 years ago. The bridge connecting two land points was to be a fishing place, a fantasy land, a place of good fish and bait smells, streetcar tracks, bait houses, sea gulls and pelicans, of dark mysterious pilings, of the exultation of catching fish, a gateway to adventure.

It was a portal where fish from the sea made their way through the pilings of the bridge to feeding spots in old Mission Bay, which was then composed of great salt marshes, sloughs, grass and a swift channel running with the tide out to sea and then with the incoming tide back again to the bay, carrying its finny burdens.

To fish, there must be bait, so the boys happily would walk into a small and odoriferous emporium of crawfish, sandy red worms apportioned in whiskey jiggers, minnows live and dead, clams, mussels and mackerel cut in bits. The crawfish were deposited in a bed of leafy seaweed in cigarette cartons. (A Chesterfield carton was supposed to bring good luck.) The home garden angleworms didn't work. For live minnows, you had to bring your own bucket.

Men in old pants, boots and plaid shirts wearing battered hats stood aside chewing tobacco in the bait shops, seemingly proud that they had furnished a full supply of bait. They were the bait-getters, and at low tides they were busy gathering clams, mussels and worms, and sucking up crawfish.

The boy yearned for the treasures on display in the bait house—the new shiny reels, the tackle boxes, knives, scalers, pliers, pole holders, snag hooks in threes, throw lines, sinkers of all weights, swivels, crab traps and more.

On the walls were photos of individuals proudly holding big fish purportedly caught off the bridge and displayed to arouse the fishing fever of the customers. They did.

The boy reluctantly left the bait house; he could have spent the day there. For over the bait tanks and counters there floated good talk of fishing—what size hooks to use, what kind of bait, the best tides, the best places on the bridge and shore, and the homely philosophies of the bait man, words of wisdom such as, "The only way a fella gets to know about fishin' is to go fishin'."

The bait and sea smells captivated him. How much better it was to be here in the bait house, dressed in an old shirt with an elastic waistband, old corduroy short pants, black cotton stockings, a greasy old cap and high copper-toed shoes, than to be in a department store all dressed up in stiff Sunday stuff.

It was the studied conclusion of the boy, reached after much consultation with his peers, that the best place to catch flounders was in shallow water. Without scientific confirmation, the lads figured live minnows were best for halibut, clams for croakers, worms for perch and smelly dead bait for sharks, especially the leopard shark, with his spectacular coloring.

The boys had heard, and they believed, that the silver mullet jumping in the bay were vegetarians which could not be caught with bait but had to be speared from a rowboat at night.

It had been decreed by some official that you must not cast with an overhead motion, lest you snag a human, an auto, a street car or your own ear. But the prohibition was not observed generally.

When anyone hooked into a big skate, all the other anglers on that side of the bridge pulled in their lines, a big gaff was obtained from a bait house and the battle to pull him to shore was on. This was a battle of man against sea monster, a battle to set the heart spinning like one of those old grind-up fishing reels.

How fast time went at the bridge. Time to clean the fish, pack them in wet sacks, give leftover bait to other fishermen and then board the street car with an adult relative—fish odors and all.

Ocean Beach was good. The bridge was marvelous. The people were good. And when the bridge was torn down in 1951, not only did the fishing go but, when the bridge died, it was like losing an old friend.

AROMAS OF YESTERDAY

There is something about fragrances and other smells that incite images of the past.

Our old barber shops, those clubby little grottos of tonsorial aromas, contributed greatly to the pleasantness of the old-time air. In those male retreats, the sunny barbers stood by their chairs in white aprons, pomaded hair parted down the middle. Their broad shoes were firmly planted on the marble floor—marble was easier to sweep than wood. Revealing mirrors and splendiferous arrays of mugs, pomades, bay rum, soap, other fragrances and white towels, hair-washing bowls and other accoutrements of the male salons provided the decor.

They were more than barber shops; they were therapy centers, too, where the man about town, hairy-chinned and hung over, came of a morning. He surrendered himself, say, to barbers Simmons and Zahler in the basement shop of the U.S. Grant Hotel. He sought rehabilitation from the wreckage of the night before, which once flamed with exuberance and stimulation and then collapsed into the cold ashes of the dawn. Trimmed, shaved, shampooed, tonicked, bay rummed, powdered and the back of his neck kneaded by some good hands, the man about town emerged in better image. Then to the Plaza Bar at 228 Broadway, or some other convenient revival spot, for a few belts to quiet the inner man before facing the world.

The sizzling of hamburgers on a grill carries with it the recollection of the delicious burgers served to the after-the-dance crowd in those years at Effie's on lower Broadway, Slim's on University Avenue, Gaby's at Old Mission Beach and Katherine's on El Cajon Boulevard, near State College.

The air seemed so much better in those days—the clean pure water of the bay, the smogless skies, the new hay in the stables, coffee-grinding stands, cigar stands exuding aromatic tobacco fumes, and the home gardens and sagebrush hills not far away.

Of course, there were some historic stinks, too, like the old hide houses near Ballast Point, the potash factory at the waterfront during World War II, the garbage scows en route to their ocean dumping grounds, horse manure and the guano boats. When the wind was from the south, the waterfront canneries expelled offensive odors that wafted over downtown, and you had to be a robust trencherman to describe them merely as the rich aromas of sardine or tuna oils.

The smell of the sea on wood invariably recalls to some old-timers the great log rafts which were floated and tugged from the Oregon coast to the Benson Lumber Co. at the foot of Sigsbee Street. The rafting started in the early 1900s and kept going for years. "The only lumber made in San Diego," Benson boasted.

From those huge trunks of Douglas fir came sawdust, and sawdust, with its clean, woodsy smells led directly to Hardy's Meat Markets. The main store was at 705 Fifth. There, huge sides of beef hung from hooks over a sawdust floor, pie-fresh to the nose, the aroma flavored by the scent of the pickle barrels.

These are but a few of the royal smells belonging to old San Diego's Great Register of Fragrances.

TENT CITY

The sea breezes of summer carry us back to barefoot days, to that dreamy little striped-canvas playland known as Coronado Tent City.

Boyville and Girlville by the bay, surf and sand, sleeping beneath the jolly canvas, no school, hot dogs and cotton candy, sliding down the slide into the pool called John Spreckels' Bathtub, droopy bathing suits smelling of moth balls, girls in swim suits, all this added up to a vacation that was just plain swell.

People today have been surfeited with more sophisticated vacations at distant places. But in a simpler age, among simpler things, there were happy days at the Tent City before the horizons of recreation were stretched afar by planes and cars. San Diegans then did not have to look far way for a vacation land. They had only to peer across the bay to the Silver Strand south of the majestic Hotel del Coronado to a sea of canvas tents, where now high-rises vie with the hotel for magnificence.

San Diegans pitched their own tents on the Strand in the real old days. Then in 1901, John D. Spreckels, San Diego's Mr. Bountiful, opened Tent City south of the great hotel. He ran street-car tracks from the hotel down the middle of the tent town, which almost immediately captured the fancy of people who felt they could not afford the hotel or who preferred a vacation under canvas with the tent set.

It was a haven for the heat-bound people of the Imperial Valley and Arizona. Some spent the whole summer in one of John D.'s tents, and loved it. They paid $27 a week for a better tent, which may have had a thatched roof, a choice location, more space, solid floors and a parlor atmosphere. But most tenters were strangers to luxury. One plain electric light bulb hung down from the center of each of the modest canvas huts and there was a gasoline stove for cooking. It was a miracle that the tent town was not wiped out by fire. Cloth curtains hung on heavy fish line provided privacy. There was a three-legged washstand and basin, a pitcher and an uncertain mirror that flung back disappointing images. The trolley roared by, the canvas walls flapped, your neighbors snored, partied and hollered, and you could hear it all clearly.

The noisy tenant whose howling after hours, sometimes powered by booze, disturbed vacationers seeking repose was politely handed a card that read, "Please be quiet." A private police patrolman who would visit offenders would do this.

It was mostly fun but it required patient adjustment to sand, sand fleas, close quarters, wet bathing suits, pickup meals and cots like rock piles.

The villain in paradise was the sinister stingaree, a non-edible flat fish that lurked half-buried in the sand of the relatively low surf of the Strand. There it speared unsuspecting bathers on the feet or ankles with poisonous barbed tail, causing painful wounds. The authorities tried galloping horses in the shallows to chase the stingrays away, but it didn't work for long.

A wide boardwalk and promenade was flanked by Glorietta Bay and the midway, which was lined with concessions. A dance pavilion was built, and on balmy summer evenings young sports in straw hats squired their girls for hours of waltzes and fox trots. A shell-shaped structure facing the bay was built for band concerts in the afternoons and evenings. Nearby was an arcade with shops, a cafeteria and a grocery store.

A bull-voiced concession huckster would wait until the final applause died down at the bandstand and then in the quiet you would inevitably hear his raucous bellow ringing out, "All right, folks. Win a ham here. Step right up."

Tent City exists today only in memory. The old arcade vanished. The Japanese tea room is gone. The palm-thatched huts were torn down. The cabins were sold and hauled away to Jacumba and Julian. There is no boardwalk. Much of Tent City was torn down when Highway 78 was routed through the cabins.

The proliferation of autos and campers and the desire of people to travel farther away for their vacations spelled doom to colorful, wonderful Tent City.

SURF FISHING

San Diegans will never know how many visitors and settlers have been attracted to these bountiful shores by the love of pole-and-reel fishing.

There were the sea, the sun, the warmth, the blue skies, the bays and the balmy breezes to draw settlers from all points on the map, and the promise of a new and more comfortable life in this Pacific paradise. And then there was the attraction of fishing.

Corvina, croaker, halibut, jack smelt, bass, perch, pompano, tuna and many other finny neighbors off our shores have helped make "compleat" anglers of San Diego sports fishermen.

"Come on out, the fishing's fine!" a new San Diegan

wrote to a friend back home. What a lure to a Nebraska snowbound angler!

Some of the first tentative steps were taken in the years from 1910 through 1920 onto fishing piers in San Diego Bay—the Lumber Wharf, the Coal Bunkers Wharf, the Coronado Pier and some smaller piers. There was a time when local fishermen caught an impressive variety of toothsome fish in San Diego Bay, but the introduction of oils, sewage and other pollutants reduced the fish supply.

In the 1920s and 30s, local fishermen could take a boat out to a fishing barge moored outside the bay in the ocean, and sample some deep-sea sport furnished by the yellowtail, barracuda, albacore and other deep-sea denizens.

From San Diego's early days, charter and public sport fishing boats loaded with happy anglers have chugged out of the harbor to fishing grounds off Point Loma and La Jolla, or near the Coronado Islands.

But, best of all, newcomers soon discovered, were the delights of surf fishing. An evening of surf fishing—what a memory!

The Mister took his entire family to the beach with the makings of a supper. If he was successful, they had a fish fry. They learned that corvina (some spell it corbina), freshly caught in the surf, was a dish fit for a gourmet. The men used long poles stuck in the sand. Sometimes the poles had bells on them to notify the angler that he had a fish on the line.

Some surf fishermen filled small Bull Durham tobacco sacks with sand and used them as sinkers in the rolling surf. Lanterns and campfires dotted the beach in the summer nights. There was room for all. Some of the men wore high fishing waders and stood in shallow waters to cast their leaders well beyond the surf line.

There is something thrilling to a devout fisherman about pulling a good-sized fish from the surf onto the beach, a sensation missing from hauling up a catch from still waters.

The beach off Torrey Pines was a favorite spot for surf fishing in the past, and the fishing was good. Feeling a bite on his line, with a midsummer moon overhead silvering the water and the weather balmy, the Ike Walton of the Teens and 20s felt a tinge of sadness for his pals “back home.”

DOWNTOWN MAN

It was a sunny morning in the early 1920s, and Mr. Old-time San Diegan, also known as Downtown Man, started his customary walk from the waterfront eastward on Broadway.

First, he stopped to chat with old men, sitting like gulls perched along the bay, trying to entice jack smelt or sea trout to their hooks, baited with red worms.

The shore fishermen swapped banter with a salty old gent in a rowboat, who dragged the bay for salvage, which he sold for his living and for the upkeep of his picturesque waterfront shack, a nautical odditorium.

Fishermen spread their nets to dry and repair at the waterfront.

The grave old pelicans, standing with their usual

dignity on bayfront pilings, looked the same as they did geologic ages ago.

The sea gulls hadn't changed much either. Our man watched them and thought of the old San Diego belief that when the gulls flew inland, rain was on the way. No rain today, the birds seemed satisfied to stay close to the ocean.

The walker hesitated and turned around to gaze at the coastal steamship moored in the bay, the *S. S. Yale*—sister ship of the *S. S. Harvard*. Wonderful ships they were. Bands played and confetti flew when passengers embarked for San Francisco.

We call our stroller Downtown Man because he lived near downtown and spent much of his time there. You couldn't get more downtown than that.

A locomotive huffed and puffed on the tracks alongside the handsome Santa Fe depot.

The stroll up Broadway turned up a few characters. We had them downtown then, too. One man hated cars and could be seen spitting on them and kicking their tires. Another wouldn't step on a crack in the sidewalk and walked carefully to avert disaster. A barefooted street orator hollered a sermon as he walked alone. Across the street a stooper worked overtime. His kind were seen mostly at night, walking along the curbs with their heads craned gutterward, searching, always searching, for purses or money dropped by careless or intoxicated motorists as they emerged from their cars. And there was a trash can prowler, picking through the rubbish barrels for food or treasure.

Foghorn blasts on the bay made their way up

Broadway. It was sunny downtown but a fog bank hung over Coronado and the entrance channel.

There, on the left, was the old county courthouse, built in 1871-72 at Front Street and Broadway on land donated by Alonzo Horton, a most venerable edifice. It was torn down in 1959, and a new courthouse was built. During its long and distinguished career, that old courthouse cradled thousands of musty documents revealing human dramas of love, hate, greed and kindness.

San Diego was emerging from its village cocoon of the 1920s. City sounds rose in the air—the clang of fire engines, the piercing bell of the police Black Maria on its way to jail, newsies hollering headlines on the corners. "Get your paper here, read all about it!" An airplane buzzed overhead, drawing glances upward from pedestrians. There was the whistle of a traffic cop, a car's horn going "aw-oo-gah," the rattle of a streetcar going by, a Victrola in a shop playing ragtime.

But, defying the auto age, an ancient horse-drawn Chinese laundry wagon slowly clop-clopped its way across Broadway to the south, to its soap and suds and mysterious markings of bundles.

On Second, just south of Broadway, the drama of newspapers hitting the streets was boisterously enacted, just like in the movies. Delivery trucks parked in the street outside the Union-Tribune dock, while the big presses thundered down below. Loaded with papers, the trucks deployed swiftly to carrier boys throughout the city, while the downtown newsies tucked their bundles under their arms and started yelling headlines immediately.

The lucky population in 1920 was 74,683. It was the rosy dawn of a grand decade.

PROHIBITION

The warnings were out, the bars closed down, the liquor shelves were bare, the drys were jubilant. Prohibition settled down over San Diego.

But Prohibition in San Diego, it soon developed, was not the same as Prohibition in many other places in the United States—not because San Diegans were more bibulous, but because of their location next to wet Mexico and their easy access to wine grapes.

If a San Diegan thirsted for store liquor, he could drive to Tijuana, put his feet on a brass rail just like the old days in San Diego, and quaff and quaff without ever having to look over his shoulder for federal agents. During part of Prohibition, the border gate to Mexico was closed each night at 6 and didn't open until the next morning, but tolerant border officials looked the other way as Tijuana-bound and homebound drinkers, both men and women, crawled through holes in the international border fence east of the main gate. Prohibition brought an economic boom to tiny Tijuana; by 1926, 75 bars were flourishing.

San Diegans, too, could tap sources of imported booze from Rum Row, off Ensenada, and enjoy the hard stuff right off the boat, a speedy rumrunner dashing to the beaches here with a load from a mother ship off Baja California.

All this, of course, was not in the foresight of the typical San Diegan who stocked up on bottled goods to the limit of his purse and his liquor cellar or closet space in anticipation of Prohibition, enacted by the 18th Amendment to the U.S. Constitution, a noble experiment to legislate morality which took effect Jan. 16, 1920.

San Diego did not know then that Prohibition would last for almost 14 years, that the city would in that time witness fantastic turns in the liquor traffic, in American mores and in respect for a major law of the land. The changes helped cause a social and economic upheaval. Some Victorian restraints were drowned in the deluge of illicit booze.

There soon opened a generous scattering of speakeasies around this Heaven on Earth. They were identified in the city directory as clubs, baths, offices, business or ordinary residences and they went by such names as Oscar's, Rena's, Joe's, Pete's and Mac's. Every town had at least one speak named Mac's. One beer place east of town went by the name of "Pipeline Nellie's." Drinks were usually 35 cents, a bottle of beer was 25 cents, and there was no free lunch.

One place here had a cigar stand out front, a bookmaking middle and a speakeasy rear, with a Rube Goldberg contraption to dump all bottles quickly if the feds got through to the back.

The bootlegger got his name from moonshiners of old who would fill their long boots with bottles of liquid corn on the way to their customers. San Diego bootleggers wore no boots and made their runs across the border in boats, but sometimes landed in jail when the feds would greet one of the boats as it beached here or intercept one of the trucks rolling north or east from the beaches with their contraband.

Meanwhile, there came a gurgling and bubbling from hundreds of crocks of home-brew beer and vats of homemade wine. No census was taken as to how many homes in San Diego had their own kitchen breweries, but the sales of malt, barley, hops, bottles, crocks, caps, capping devices and other paraphernalia of the brew-meisters suggest that they were numerous.

Vineyard owners here and in the San Joaquin Valley, who had feared bankruptcy with the coming of Prohibition, reported gains in income because of the clause in the law which permitted householders to make a certain amount of home wine for their own use. It seems some of this was sold.

Federal agents were baffled. One said, "The attempt to stop people from making their own liquor and selling it on a small scale is impossible."

San Diegans ruminating over what reform may take root next might remember there was talk of outlawing such wicked dances as the tango, hesitation waltz, bunny hug, turkey trot, shimmy, sea-gull swoop, camel walk and the skunk waltz.

TIJUANA IN THE 20s

An unchaperoned visit to old Tijuana by San Diego boys and girls in the 1920s was an adventure—the blare of saloons, booze, painted girls, souvenirs, hawkers, barkers, squalor and excitement.

The unauthorized trip to Tijuana was most likely in defiance of parent admonitions that the Mexican border town held dangers and pitfalls for the young. But some went anyway, impelled by curiosity, peer pressure and those mysterious forces that move youth to ignore the advice of elders. They drove the 17 miles to T-town in a Model T Ford.

The flivver and its laughing load made it through the towns of National City and Chula Vista on its southward route before approaching the gate, a drab-looking portal then. The Model T rumbled onto the old Tijuana Bridge, and the boys and girls stared with mixed emotions at the squalor beneath, near the river. They saw shacks, some made from packing boxes, women with children washing clothes in the river, and signs of dire poverty all around. Some sensitive and sympathetic souls felt twinges of guilt at the contrast between the river people, struggling for existence, and American kids with pocketfuls of money bound for drinking, dancing and flirting with vice.

Just across the bridge there was a forest of billboards and smaller signs. Some advertised quick marriages and divorces. A crowd of people wound slowly up and down Avenida Revolucion, the main street. Vendors, from small boys to old women, hawked goods ranging from homemade cakes to packages of gum. Some boys lugged around shoeshine boxes, begging Americans to have their shoes shined for a very low price. Any American with a heart tipped them generously, no matter the quality of the shine.

The flivver was parked on a side street. The kids went to a small cart, stationed just off Avenida Revolucion, for tacos. Their taco man had a way with tortillas and he filled them with delicious interiors. Before the trip started, the youth grapevine in San Diego had been tapped on where to go in Tijuana.

Next, they went to what was billed as "The Longest Bar in the World." It was indeed, a long bar. Opposite the bar was a wall of fun-house mirrors. The bravest boys bought a generous shot of tequila, with a beer chaser, for 15 cents, and the girls giggled at their reflections in the crazy mirrors.

To get at least a peek at sin, the young visitors went to the open door of the Moulin Rouge, a famous brothel, and furtively peered at girls sitting around inside. Later, the place was moved down a hill from the Avenida to a palace of sin.

Shopping lured Americans young and old, men and women. They bought Irish linen, French perfume, serapes, leather sandals, sombreros, blouses and skirts, copper pots, piñatas, baskets and silver objects. The clang of cash registers vied with the marimba bands for the attention of tourists. Plaintive Mexican ballads came in great waves from open saloon doors. Barkers outside cabarets promised nude shows inside.

It seemed then that all the cacophony of the Southwest had been poured into the jumping, sparkling, howling and bustling little town of Tijuana. Prohibition had opened the floodgates of tourism from the United States and Tijuana was ready for the big party. Tijuana streets stretched out to new lengths as the bars sprang up. Long lines of Tijuana-bound cars jammed the highways to the border. Hollywood celebrities joined the rush and helped make Tijuana world-famous as a capital of fun and freedom.

The Foreign Club, a lavish restaurant, bar and gambling place, drew the well-to-do and well-dressed visitors.

The girls and boys of the Model T carried small Spanish-English dictionaries to try their high school Spanish on the natives.

"Buenos dias, señor. ¿Como está usted?"

"Just fine, buddy. How are you?"

A short way out of town Mexican craftsmen squatted on the ground and made shoes and sandals and wove serapes. It all seemed more Mexican and foreign then—the more exciting, good old, bad old Tijuana of the 20s.

CALIENTE'S HEYDAY

Poverty and dazzling luxury lived side by side in Tijuana in the late 1920s and early 30s. Agua Caliente sparkled as the plush playground of the rich. But across the valley of the Tia Juana River you might have seen the crude hovel of a Mexican goatherd whose weekly sustenance wouldn't have equaled the price of a round of golf at the Caliente course.

San Diegans were beauty-struck on their first visit to Caliente. They were able to mingle with the rich and beautiful people of the world. They were awe-struck at the astounding amounts of money flung over the gambling tables. They filled their eyes with opulence and their stomachs with gourmet viands and the best of liquors, escaping from the puritanical restrictions of Prohibition which had been imposed then on the U.S. side of the border.

Brilliantly plumaged tropical birds flew around the garden. The grounds were spotless, neatly kept and always green—the color of American currency. The rooms of the individual bungalows and the hotel were luxurious. The restrooms were elegant.

In the Gold Room, or *Salon de Oro,* patrons who could afford it played roulette, craps, poker, blackjack, faro, chuck-a-luck, slot machines—everything. Tables dazzled with $10, $20 and $30 gold coins instead of chips. High rollers won and lost fortunes in gold.

Prices, though, were relatively moderate. In 1930, room rates were $5, $6, $8, $10 and $12, European plan. "Also suites and romantic Spanish villas" were advertised, "where the doors to romance open!" Luncheon at the casino patio cost only $1 weekdays and $1.50 weekends. Friday nights were college nights, with dinner, wine and a floor show for $1 a person.

Maybe your dinner entertainment might have been the lovely Rita Cansino, dancing as a teen-ager with her father in an act billed as "The Cansinos." You would recognize her later as the Hollywood star, Rita

Hayworth.

The resort attracted the famous people of stage, screen, business and the professions. Celebrities from foreign countries and sports played there, as well as some of the notorious bigwigs of crime. The racketeer Al Capone was said to have occupied a chair in the Gold Room once. And among others who stayed and played were Charles Chaplin, Al Jolson, Sid Grauman, Jean Harlow, Lupe Velez, Delores Del Rio, Jackie Coogan and Harold Lloyd, all from Hollywood, plus Babe Ruth and the auto racer Barney Oldfield. Rumors of scandalous doings by the rich and famous in the plush resort crossed the border.

Seasoned newsmen, describing the luxuries of Caliente, soon found themselves vending outrageous fluff. Wrote one:

"Sixteen miles from San Diego, one of America's most beautiful cities, the American finds here everything that he could find at Deauville, Monte Carlo, Nice or any other resort in Europe. This place is extraordinarily beautiful, with a perfect hotel, golf, and hot sulphur and mud baths famous in Aztec days. The visitor is in old Mexico, a land as foreign to him and as fascinating as if he were in Spain, yet near his own land, no ocean to cross."

The author: conservative columnist Arthur Brisbane.

Some high rollers complained because the casino was closed from 5 a. m. to 10 a. m. daily.

It all came to an end July 20, 1935, when gambling at Agua Caliente and all other Mexican casinos was banned by order of Mexican President Lazaro Cardenas.

The race track kept going but the glittering resort faded away. Prohibition was repealed in the United States and the diners and the dancers, the drinkers and the gamblers moved on to other places, other dreams.

MISSION BEACH BALLROOM

The old Mission Beach Ballroom was a splendid palace of terpsichore.

The ballroom was built in 1925 by John D. Spreckels, San Diego's bountiful benefactor, as part of the $4 million Mission Beach Amusement Center. The ballroom was popular during the 20s, 30s and 40s.

When it closed, there was sadness among those who had spent many nights of dancing over the extra-fine maple floor.

The gala opening was in 1925, on the 75th anniversary of California's admission to the Union in 1850. Today, the ballroom is no more. It was razed some time after it closed, and its place on the shore is occupied, in part, by the lifeguard headquarters. Soft music no longer drifts from its great oval.

Couples, standing on the esplanade outside the ballroom, enjoyed a romantic atmosphere created by a bright half moon marking a silver trail on the water, the surf singing a ragged song of the sea and soft night breezes drifting to shore. A lot of marriage proposals were offered in that tender setting.

Inside, there was dreamy music in the air, star-like mirrored lights sparkled from above and the magnificence of the great hall cast a romantic spell upon the dancers, the young men with pretty girls in their arms. Was there ever a finer evening for a lad and lass than this?

The elegant dance palace rose from verbena-covered sand dunes to its heights of splendor. It came when San Diego and the rest of the country were prosperous and the future looked bright. Who, dancing cheek to cheek with his best girl, could foretell the dark Depression years ahead?

Spreckels extended his electric railway line from Ocean Beach through Mission Beach and thence to La Jolla. The channel was spanned by a wooden bridge from Ocean Beach to Mission Beach, a traffic-way which also served as a makeshift fishing pier. for small boys and old men holding poles in their hands.

Spreckels believed he could create the recreational center of the West, another Venice in America. Eventually, the amusement center was given to the city of San Diego. The dancing casino was the centerpiece of the complex of amusement games and rides, including the roller coaster called the Giant Dipper, which still stands as a skeleton of the fun-filled past.

It cost 25 cents to get into the ballroom, more if a big band was playing, and 25 cents more if you engaged a loge to sit in. On Friday nights, the ballroom put on Campus Capers at bargain rates for the college crowd.

Single men and single girls went to the casino and got in plenty of dancing. The boys asked the girls, introduced or not, and away they went! The boy had to buy the tickets—five cents for each dance, which lasted five minutes. Young men took your tickets at one of the gates to the floor. You had plenty of room to whirl and twirl and swing your partners; the hall was huge. The handsome, tanned lifeguards could be spotted flitting around the floor. Some young men got their early dance schooling at the ballroom, much to the pain of some girls.

"I didn't know he couldn't dance!"

The bandstand was lighted by various spotlights, and the worshiping fans crowded around the front of the stand to pay tribute to famous leaders and vocalists. Big bands like those led by Tommy Dorsey, Phil Harris, Guy Lombardo, Ted Fio Rito and Glen Miller played the ballroom.

Sometimes tiny crepe-paper parachutes flooded to the floor through a deluge of lights. Attached to some were gifts, such as passes to the hall. This innocent surprise never failed to elicit shouts of excitement, as the ceiling flickered with many colors.

When the surfside palace fell to dust and rubble, some saw the shadows of remembered loves and friends, dancing cheek to cheek as the ghostly echoes of "Good night, sweetheart, 'til we meet tomorrow" played the last dance.

THE ROARING 20s

The Roaring 20s weren't all bad, all good, all sheiks and flappers, all bathtub gin or all sex. The city gained on several fronts in a 20s boom, and the decade was interesting, and full of initiative, vision and accomplishment.

But the jazz decade is ever remembered, at costume and gin parties, for its flappers with bobbed hair, shockingly short skirts, silk stockings rolled below the knees and low-cut tops, doing the Charleston with boys wearing bell-bottomed trousers, shiny leather shoes, and three-button coats, their hair greased slick like Rudolph Valentino's. You could tell a boy from a girl, even though the shebas tried to achieve the flat-lath look.

The young people resented any suggestion that their deviations from what was believed to be the old norms should subject them to psychiatric examination. They were not afraid of tomorrow, for they had had a glimpse of yesterday, and they loved today.

New people came to San Diego, in wave after wave, as its allurements were praised in roseate rhetoric from the San Diego California Club. Most everything that happened here that got national attention ballyhooed the many charms of this jewel by the sea.

In the dawn of the decade, the world turned its eyes on San Diego in 1920, when His Royal Highness, the Prince of Wales, later King Edward VIII, was royally entertained here.

In 1927, Charles Lindbergh stepped off to take delivery of a plane made for him here by Ryan Air Service, a plane called "The Spirit of St. Louis," in which he made his historic solo flight across the Atlantic to France. "Clap hands, here comes Charlie," the townsfolk sang and chanted when he returned here for a huge welcome and celebration.

In 1926, three queens of the movies—Norma, Constance and Natalie Talmadge—swept into town to open a new subdivision, Talmadge Park, out Adams Avenue way.

The handsome Spreckels Building on Broadway between First and Second was on its way up. San Diego moved into peacetime military importance with the establishment of the Marine Corps Recruit Depot in 1921 and the Naval Training Center in 1923. In 1922, the Navy dedicated its new hospital in Balboa Park.

The waterfront bustled with new prosperity. The value of cargo shipping rose dramatically.

In 1925 the Mission Beach Amusement Center opened, featuring a large bathhouse plunge, which is still here, a dancing casino, since torn down, and an esplanade and seawall 1,600 feet long. It wasn't long before the boys and girls were hoofing tirelessly, cheek to cheek, in the ballroom to such velvety dandies as "Always" or flipping and flapping to the more frenetic "Charleston," "Varsity Drag" or "Muskrat Ramble."

Aimee Semple McPherson appeared in a black velvet gown trimmed with white lace to preach at the Organ Pavilion in Balboa Park.

Mahjong and the Eskimo Pie became fads.

Some of the newcomers who flocked here for the sun and sea were jobless or didn't have adequate funds, so employment and welfare problems loomed in paradise.

We may never again see such a decade, though. Everyone was young, or seemed like it. Money was plentiful and getting more plentiful, or so it seemed, as the 20s roared to an end.

Then came 1929.

Crash!

DEATH OF A NEWSPAPER

In January 1928, I experienced the sad drama of the final edition of a daily newspaper. The San Diego Independent, a short-lived sheet, breathed its last when it was bought and publication was discontinued.

It was my first job on a daily newspaper, so the emotions ran deep that last night in the small paper-strewn editorial room. I was still a teen-ager and felt the demise much more than veterans of the staff.

One staffer had only four more stops to go before he would have read copy in every state in the country. It was a time of wandering newspaper reporters and deskmen who, after landing a job, began writing applications in search of another one.

That last night, gag headlines were pasted all over the city room, such as, "Here today, gone tomorrow," "Join the Navy and see the world," "Indigents reach new low in San Diego," "Help wanted" and "Don't slam the door as you leave."

Over my desk had been pasted an excerpt from a journalism school primer to the effect that journalism is, at best, a precarious career. Most of the reporters had applied for new jobs elsewhere.

As the presses rolled, the reporters, cubs and veterans, cleaned out their desks of notes, pencils, erasers, scissors and other tools of the trade.

There was a farewell party at the home of one of the employees. A few of the staff members went downtown later to have a last look at the messy city room.

Being young and sensitive, I wondered if Tom Berry, the telegraph editor, who was an older man, would land another job. He was my idol. I once wrote that "Mr. Berry was a journalistic gentleman of the old guard, whose likes from a robust era were fast dropping into the pages of history." I copied his fashion of wearing a green eye shade. His clothing, even on a steaming hot summer night, was impeccable, from his shiny high shoes to his white shirt and neatly knotted cravat. His pencils were neatly arrayed alongside his left arm and his search for lead stories that last night was as zealous as ever.

I don't know what happened to him. Some of the editorial staffers eventually landed jobs on the other newspapers in town—the Union or the Tribune or the Sun. I got a job on the Sun.

One who missed the pain of that last night at the Independent had lost his job earlier. He was called Biv and that's all I knew him by. He was the telegraph operator. He presided over his key and translated the mysterious dots and dashes of the incoming news stories onto his Underwood typewriter. He punctuated his operations with spats of tobacco juice into an old cuspidor.

Biv roundly cussed the new teletype machines, the technological innovation which eventually cost him his job. If some of his tobacco juice splashed on them, it wasn't accidental.

I never heard whether Biv got another job or not. Technological unemployment was a new kind of American drama.

THE BLUE FLYER

A little ghost from the past came puttering down the freeway the other day—the obvious pride of its owners. My mind flew back to the wonderful Blue Flyer, in which I once had a personal interest.

The Blue Flyer was neither a true blue nor could it fly; it wasn't a Cadillac but it wasn't an ox cart. It was a Model T, like the one driving in front of me, the sturdy and reliable low-priced product of Henry Ford, who put many thousands of Americans on wheels.

In the late 1920s, when the Model T was being phased out in favor of the Model A, San Diego students traveled by land and by sea to their colleges up north.

If by sea, they probably went aboard either the *Yale* or the *Harvard*, the popular coastal steamers. If by land, the trip might have been made in a Model T roadster, like the Blue Flyer.

Travel across California in the 20s was an adventure, and in a Model T it was excitement, rugged pleasure and a challenge. Some parents in San Diego thought it was foolhardy for two young men to embark in an old Model T to drive to Berkeley and the University of California, a distance of some 500 miles.

The Blue Flyer, so named by its admiring owners, could go 45 miles an hour maximum, and get about 22 miles on a gallon of gas. It didn't gobble up the miles as it rolled merrily along, but took them steadily and quite smoothly. It had no radio, no air conditioning, no automatic shift, no mechanical windshield wipers, no self-starter—none of those improvements hovering in the future. But the Blue Flyer waited patiently at the curb for its intrepid owners—Frank and Arthur Ribbel, brothers and students at UC.

It really wasn't necessary for our friends and neighbors to give us such an effusive farewell. After all, we weren't going to the Pole, even though we did feel like pioneers.

It was late April, and the weather was ideal. Daylight stayed a long time, and although the headlights were not powerful, the Flyer kept going at night, helped by bright moonlight. The small Ford chugged up and down the hills, over the Ridge Route, through the valleys and small towns. While one drove, the other dozed.

There were filling stations along the way. There was a wooden stick to measure the amount of gas that remained in the tank. There were few road signs and few road maps.

There were great fields of wildflowers, especially off the long stretch leading into Bakersfield. Poppy fields were ablaze. Rabbit, quail and dove were in great numbers.

Because the old Model T didn't go very fast, its occupants had time to enjoy the landscape. And to buy a jug of bootleg wine near Bakersfield.

At long last, Berkeley appeared, and we rolled down College Avenue, where our fraternity house was located. The brothers were out front ready to welcome us and give us that mystic grip. They couldn't believe that we had driven so far without even one flat tire.

The Blue Flyer was famous! And the wine helped celebrate its triumph.

SISTER SHIPS

Since 1911—with a break during World War I—the 21-knot steamer *Harvard* and its sister ship, the *Yale*, had been plying between San Diego, Los Angeles and San Francisco, providing the traveling public with metropolitan luxury and such pleasures as dance bands and lavish buffets, along with performing the more mundane task of hauling freight.

For collegians sailing to and from their schools north of here, everything aboard the *Harvard* and *Yale* seemed all new, all good; all was well with the world. Younger passengers hoped there were many members of the opposite sex aboard. Romances began to bloom as soon as the ship rounded Point Loma and headed north.

Imagine the start of a trip in those carefree days. You are ready to embark on a 25-hour cruise to San Francisco. A lively band plays on deck. Passengers stream up the gangplank, hand their luggage to the stewards—except for the suitcases that gurgle and clink with bootleg bottles—and line the rail to wave goodbye to friends on the Broadway Pier. The plank is pulled up, the ship moves slowly away, and confetti and colored streamers float away toward the stern.

The standard stateroom provided a closet, a wash basin and two berths, one up and one down. If you didn't have a roommate, you had to share with a stranger.

There were four sailings weekly, at 9 a. m. The fare was as low as $8 one way to San Francisco and $14 round trip. That included food and the entertainment featured dancing the night away.

And what food! Your hungry collegians reveled in cheese, canapés, olives, celery, *potage du jour,* consommé, fried yellowtail with tartar sauce, roast leg of spring lamb, broiled sirloin steak Bordelaise, French carrots, cauliflower hollandaise, hearts of lettuce, pie, pears, small cakes, ice cream, toasted wafers and *café noir.* And then you better not get seasick.

The southbound *Harvard* came to a sad end just before dawn on May 30, 1931, when it ran on the rocks in heavy fog at Point Arguello, north of Santa Barbara. The place was called the graveyard of the Pacific. It was where seven U.S. Navy destroyers ran aground en masse in 1923. About 500 *Harvard* passengers took to the lifeboats and were rescued by the Navy cruiser *USS Louisville*, which took them safely to San Pedro. There was no loss of life, but the good ship *Harvard* was a total loss.

Five years later, the *Yale* suspended service. During World War II, the Navy used it for a houseboat in the Aleutians.

When the ships started their runs, San Diego boasted only about 40,000 people. The currently jammed and dangerous freeways from San Diego north elicit in the hearts and minds of some oldsters a sincere wish to revive the sailings of the *Yale* and *Harvard*.

DEPRESSION

As far as is known, no best seller entitled *The College Boy and the Depression* has ever hit the bookshelves in our town, yet the suffering of this young man during the blue decade was very real and, to him, no romp. He had lived the life of campus and fraternity for four abundant years, and the descent into the economic morass was painfully abrupt.

But the college boy's woe never dropped to the distressing level of the husband with a family to feed, a harried housewife trying to make a dollar stretch and stretch, an unemployed person searching fruitlessly for work, the indigent, homeless, moneyless and elderly.

The college boy had heard some rumblings of the Depression while still on campus, through letters from home and by reading the newspapers, but he was isolated from the real misery and thus his shock was delayed. He had been warned. At his graduation exercises in 1932 at Berkeley, Robert Gordon Sproul, the university president, solemnly told the graduating seniors that they would be faced with the worst economic conditions in the history of the university.

But jolly Senior Week festivities washed away his worries and then he boarded the coastwise vessel *Emma Alexander* at San Francisco for the trip home. The dinner he ate aboard was the most sumptuous he would have for some time. He landed in San Diego with $1.85 in his pocket and part of that went for streetcar fare home.

The marks of the Depression were on the faces of his worried parents and his sister. San Diego had not been hit as hard as many Eastern places, because it wasn't a one-industry town where all business stopped when the factory closed. And the Navy payroll here continued to rise impressively from 1929 to 1934, cushioning local businessmen from some of the economic hardship that was felt across the country. Nevertheless, the value of building permits in San Diego dropped by half in one year, and bank debits fell $100 million. In 1932, 16,000 were unemployed out of a population of 223,000. There were 4,000 families on relief. And the next year the unemployed rose to 23,000. About a tenth of the population was jobless and looking for work. Five-room houses were selling for $3,000. Smaller homes were offered for $1,500, with few buyers.

There were more beggars and panhandlers on downtown streets. Soup lines began to form. “Hoover-villes,” the shack towns of the poor, were built of packing boxes, scrap iron, wood and discards on the fringes of town and near the city dumps. To keep warm, people built fires in empty oil drums. Homeless people huddled in downtown doorways at night. Scavengers poked through the garbage cans in the alleys outside restaurants. Some transients slept in their cars.

There were many more hitchhikers, as people moved vainly about looking for jobs. Hobos swarmed over the freight trains, riding the rails.

At the homes of the more affluent, servants were let go and then were hired back for room and board, no pay.

Vacant stores made sad gaps in business blocks downtown. Prominent businessmen who had preached the doctrine of rugged individualism considered themselves lucky to get jobs with the WPA, the Works Progress Administration, a keystone of President Franklin D. Roosevelt's New Deal. Others were accepting menial jobs. One businessman exulted when he finally landed a job paying $70 a month.

Marriages were postponed until the groom could get work. Boys took their girls out on cheap dates, perhaps a walk to the movies with a nickel Coke on the way home. Homeowners put off needed repairs and a newly painted house was rarely seen.

Our young man used a mechanical roller gadget to roll cigarettes from scratch when ready-made cigarettes became a luxury. His father became adept at halfsoling shoes in the basement. Many families were buying home haircut kits and cutting their own hair. Do it yourself or make do. If you can't eat it or wear it, don't buy it. Those were Depression watchwords.

It was reported some desperate men were rustling calves from ranches in the back country.

Our young man discovered that his pals felt lucky to be pumping gas in filling stations. Some Ph.D.s went to work at the gas pumps. Drivers might buy only 35 cents' worth of gas at a time.

Prices were low—hamburger, 5 cents a pound, potatoes, 10 cents a pound, eggs, 32 cents a dozen, coffee, 15 cents a pound, pork and beans, 5 cents a can.

There simply wasn't any money around. After the bank failures some folks buried their cash in jars in the back yard, or behind bricks in unused chimneys.

But quiet bravery was shown. Families came closer together. Grown children returned to their old homesteads and shared the diminished bounty with the old folks. In-laws moved in together. Neighbors helped each other and lent necessities to each other. One silk maternity dress made the rounds among friends until it was threadbare.

Beans, wild game, fresh-caught fish, home-grown vegetables and homemade bread were menu standards.

Slowly, oh so slowly, San Diego clambered out of the Depression. The "college" of our college boy wore off fast. The happy day came at last when he found a job. He married his sweetheart, worked his way out of the hole and fought his way through World War II, like so many of his generation.

THE 1935-1936 EXPO

The 1935 California Pacific International Exposition in San Diego was a grand party. It was an escape from the gray gloom of the 1930s, it was a place to go, a stein song, a merry-go-round, an education. It was starlight, excitement, movement and a generous offering of attractions. It was also a daring enterprise in the black core of the Depression.

Even the name was impressive. It opened on May 29, 1935, and closed on Nov. 11. It was reopened the next year on Feb. 12 and ran until Sept. 9. But the Expo's second year did not have the exuberance of 1935 or the success. Some exhibitors had pulled out, and competition was felt from other fairs elsewhere in the country.

The earlier 1915-1916 Panama California Exposition was new and beautiful, stately and dignified, but it didn't have the zing of the 1935-1936 spectacular.

Many visitors started their day at the Expo with a visit to the Nudist Colony. Some of the nudists came here from a similar attraction at the Chicago World's Fair of the year before. Several dozen girls and a few well-along men lolled about the scene, named Zoro Gardens and located in the northern section of the sylvan gulch near the Pepper Grove in Balboa Park. Zoro was a fictitious sun deity.

King Zoro, the colony's leader, and the other men had long beards and wore bathing trunks. The women wore brassieres and G-strings. In fact, the nudists weren't nude. None was as bare as the beach-goers of the 1980s. Police Chief George Sears saw to it that the fair performers wore enough clothes to pass the test of modesty. But even so, a group of local citizens filed their objections with the City Council, which decided not to close the popular and lucrative exhibit.

The colony was a prime target for sailors and male civilians under 100 visiting the Expo. The ticket line also included some handsome, dignified old grandmas and grandpas with naughty looks.

What American could fret about the Depression while ogling Queen Zorine or Ming Toy, daintily shooting her bow and arrow?

Paunchy men attending conventions in San Diego made the colony a priority port of call. So did visiting newsmen. Stories about the colony made their way over news wires to newspaper all over the country. It was the Black's Beach of the 30s.

And there were other attractions. Gold Gulch, a simulated California gold country mining town, displayed all the trappings of the Mother Lode. Sally Rand waved her famous fans and refused to go near the Nudist Colony. So did the evangelist Aimee Semple McPherson when she visited the fair. "I only invited her to tea," said Queen Zorine. "I didn't ask her to take her clothes off."

There were educational exhibits of a serious type. At the Ford Building, which now houses the Aero-Space Museum, visitors were shown how automobiles were made. And an exhibit showed how Boulder Dam, now Hoover Dam, had just been built.

The Indian Village, built by the Santa Fe Railroad for the 1915-16 fair, was still there to attract tourists in 1935-36.

And there were pretty girls, girls, girls, everywhere, at the ticket windows, on stage, walking around the grounds.

A midway provided carnival color and spirit. There was a German beer garden at one end with waiters in leather shorts, rosy-cheeked girls and a brass band. In the "Crime Doesn't Pay" show, John Dillinger's bulletproof sedan was displayed. There was a midget village, flea circuses, freak animals, all sorts of rides, parachute jumpers, and a man who sold thousands of kazoos by barking and humming a tune on his hum-a-tune gadget.

President Franklin D. Roosevelt was an honored guest. There was a Kate Sessions Day. Madame Ernestine Schumann-Heink, the opera star whose home here gave the Grossmont area its fame, sang at the 1935-1936 Expo, as she had at the 1915-1916 Expo.

When it was all over, there was an emptiness in the park and in San Diego. The gloom clouds came back.

S. S. MONTE CARLO

The Depression spawned all sorts of money-making schemes in the 30s and the casino ship *Monte Carlo* was one of them. It was 300 feet long, a converted freighter, with a concrete hull and no engines. It was anchored three miles off Point Loma and Coronado in international waters where, it was believed, gambling would be legal or at least outside the jurisdiction of the police.

District Attorney Thomas Whelan cited a state statute prohibiting the transportation of people to gambling ships, but a Superior Court judge threw out the case, saying the prosecutor hadn't proved that gambling was conducted aboard the ship.

Let's go out in our imagination and have a look for ourselves. We have a few misgivings about the trip as we step carefully aboard a fairly large shore boat and settle in our seats as we watch the lights of the Embarcadero slide by.

The boat moves out in the harbor. The wind is cold. Spray washes over some of the passengers like a cold shower. They complain that they were not told to wear warm clothing. It's a rough trip and some of the passengers look a little green around the gills.

The boat negotiates the bay and heads out the harbor mouth into the open sea. Swells can be felt. Misgivings grow deeper and darker. Where are the life preservers, if any?

At last a great lighted hulk looms. We stand up. Getting up the gangplank takes some agility, and some older people can't make it. They stay in the boat and head back.

We are aboard the sinful *Monte Carlo*. We feel a little trapped, because we know we can't leave until the next shore boat comes, even if we want to. It seems dank in the casino, despite the lights, the people and the tables.

We can play craps, roulette, blackjack and poker, or enjoy the diversions of the dance floor, bar and food, spiced with the thrill of doing something that might be naughty.

Some of those drained by the Depression may have thought they could recoup their fortunes, but they never said how they came out. Gamblers are often silent on that subject.

"It wasn't worth the trip," growled the losers. "Too long to get there, too cold and too rough."

Who owned the ship? Some men from out of town. Whoever they were, they lost their stake on New Year's Eve, 1936.

After all the guests had left, the ship was closed for the winter. Two caretakers were left aboard. The casino was dark. Then a heavy gale hit the coast. The ship broke the anchor chain and floundered in the swells before being blown ashore and grounded broadside on the strand.

The stranded caretakers fired distress flares into the night sky and were rescued by the Coast Guard.

Beachcombers, some well-dressed, waded through shallow water and wet sand to collect gambling gew-gaws from the ship, which broke up in the surf. There was a rumor that hundreds of cases of whiskey floated ashore. No one found any bottles, or at least no one reported finding any.

THE OLD COLISEUM

A devout old boxing fan, standing alone at night at the southwest corner of 15th and E streets, might hear, from some mysterious twilight zone, the roar of the crowd, the clang of the bell, and the stir and shuffle of excited people.

Our fan would know that the Friday night fights were coming through to him from the old Coliseum, once an institution, a habit, a hobby and a night out for the he-men of our town.

It's gone now, that wonderful place. The building was sold long ago to Jerome's Furniture for use as a warehouse. But at this writing still visible through the exterior coating are the outlines of the old ticket windows which sold the ducats to the lines of fans waiting to get in.

Stand, you fight buffs, outside this venerable building and hear the echoes of the Damon Runyanesque crowd bellowing for the kill, with the shrill voices of the females intermingled with the hoarse yells of the men. "Turn out the lights, they want to be alone" for a couple of slow fighters. "Kill him, hit him with the ring post" when the going got bloody. The women were as bloodthirsty as the men. Women with escorts were admitted free. The masculine throats were well oiled with whiskey, beer, or both, to give them a more hearty pitch.

You will hear the dramatic voice of the distinguished announcer, Curly Morgan, and his image will come back to you—tall, slender, with wavy hair, the well-dressed Curly with a flower in his lapel, pointing a long finger with one foot off the ground toward one corner, then the other, introducing the fighters.

The Coliseum opened on Nov. 28, 1924. It was often filled to the rafters with about 3,500 seats sold. That was on Friday night. There were wrestling matches on Tuesdays, but the fight fans scorned them.

The smell of sweat, the thick cigarette and cigar smoke dimming the lights, the insistent clang of the bell in the expert hands of Al Lambla, the smack of leather against bone and flesh, the grunts and gasps of the gladiators and the shouted advice from managers in their corners are well remembered. Watta night!

Watta fight!

There were rubbers and corner men, managers, trainers and officials—all members of a colorful fight community that once included Jerome O'Connor, father of Mayor Maureen O'Connor.

A procession of fighters slugged through Coliseum battles. A few fought their way from here to the top. Archie Moore, the former light heavyweight champion of the world, for example. And then there were Long Tom Hawkins, Canvasback Cohen, Cowboy Charlie Cobb, the Hogue Twins and others whose names have long been forgotten.

For some, the walk in defeat back to the dressing room was a dreary descent into a career's end, their hopes for gold and glory smashed. Sometimes an old punch-drunk fighter would shuffle in, the happy recipient of a ticket from the house, and relive for an hour the glory he had won in the ring.

The fans battered the roof and ribs of the fight palace with their roars, but the old house weathered the storm.

THE SODA JERK

In the mind's gallery of images, from the days of wire-legged stools and marble drugstore counters, the bright faces of soda jerks come smiling through.

There can be no unpleasant vibration associated with the typical soda jerk, for he presided over treats and goodies and tasty bubble creations from his fountain spigots, his big cans of ice cream and his syrup jars.

There he was, Mr. America, a hat or cap of red and white tilted jauntily and holding back thick young hair, possibly blond. Blond went so well with vanilla ice cream! He was clean, clean, clean; his hands, fingernails, face, neck and ears were clean; some customers said he had a complexion like a strawberry milk shake, all pink and white. He was called a soda jerk or a soda squirt. In that more innocent age, the term jerk had not yet become a term of abuse. The dictionary defined him as: "A person who prepares and dispenses refreshments at a soda fountain."

If we could go back there in time, we could get a plain chocolate soda for five cents. It cost 10 cents if ice cream scoops were added.

Drugstores downtown and uptown in San Diego found the fountains good business, and a drugstore without a fountain was like a restaurant without dessert.

The soda jerk was an American original, and his confections were originals. The good ones had a generous formula for making ice cream sodas. First, they would put in the syrup—vanilla, chocolate or strawberry, then a hefty chunk of ice cream. They would mash the ice cream in the syrup with a long spoon. The soda water was added and two more scoops of ice cream were dropped in the mixture and the glass topped with soda to overflowing. Some drugstores added a dollop of whipped cream on top. The soda jerk was accommodating, so you could have one scoop of vanilla and one scoop of strawberry, if you chose.

"We knew the one who made the best sodas and shakes and we all went to him," one San Diego woman recalled.

The greatest production was the banana split. The

soda jerk would select a canoe-shaped dish while his customers waited and watched at the marble counter. He would deposit three large scoops of real ice cream into it, vanilla, chocolate and strawberry. Then he would pour different flavored syrups over them and decorate the dish with bananas sliced the long way, fresh peaches, and perhaps whipped cream, crushed almonds and maraschino cherries. It was beautiful. His eyes had the look of an artist who has completed a major work. You hesitated to plunge your spoon into the masterpiece.

But people did not insult soda jerks by spurning their creations, so you would eat the cherry first, then a bit of ice cream, then a bite of banana and you were on your way—the finish came so fast, so soon, and you pushed your empty dish away.

The soda jerks also had to make sandwiches of boiled ham, tuna fish, or chicken salad, but their fame rested on their phosphates, sundaes, sodas and splits, Cokes, malts and shakes.

The personable dispenser had some fringe benefits. He could make points with the girls at his counter by adding extra scoops of ice cream to their sodas and shakes. He was the caliph of confections in his neighborhood, with a repertoire that placed him high in the esteem of his peers. Anybody who could build a banana split like that could never in those years be a social pariah. Why, he even competed with licensed pharmacists, who sometimes filled in at the fountains, in making superior mixes under the soda spigots. The cheery soda jerk and charismatic squirt were the chosen ones in youthful society at the time.

The drugstore soda fountains went on the endangered list some time ago, as did the bright young soda jerks. In some remote bit of yesterday there may be preserved genuine fountains with marble counters, syrup jars and soda water, but alas, there are no soda jerks of old-time flair and freshness. They not only dispensed ice cream sodas, they spread joy.

The disappointment of yesterday's fountain sitters was keen when they first came face to face with that sad sign:

"Fountain closed."

HAMILTON'S FINE FOODS

The fine foods of Charles S. Hamilton's wonderful old San Diego grocery store still are table talk and many an old gourmet wishes the store was still alive and delivering.

Founded in 1878, it was operated by one family until the 1940s, and achieved in quality what many of today's supermarkets boast about but never attain. "It came from Hamilton's" was an assurance in older San Diego that the food was the best.

The evolution of Hamilton's started when clerks Charles S. Hamilton and George W. Marston bought out their boss, Joseph Nash, a general merchant at

Fifth and K streets. The two paid $10,000 cash for the store. At Nash's they sold codfish, molasses, coal oil, hardware, notions, clothing and chicken feed. The Hamilton-Marston partnership went on until 1878, when Marston started a department store and Hamilton launched his grocery store near Fifth and G on an unpaved street.

"Charley" would answer the phone, take orders and at the same time swap some friendly small-town chitchat with his neighbors. He was clerk, manager, owner, telephone operator, janitor and delivery man with horse and wagon. Out front he had bins and boxes of apples and other fruits, vegetables and nuts, brooms, mops, kitchen utensils and other wants.

No railroads served San Diego then. Food was brought in chiefly by sea. Sometimes there were long waits between boats. Eventually, Hamilton's imported food from nearly every part of the world, even by airplane, which impressed San Diego.

Hamilton took in a partner in 1876, when he married Elizabeth Gunn, sister of Mrs. George Marston and a member of a family prominent in early San Diego history.

Later, Hamilton moved his store to Sixth and C streets, across from George Marston's great department store. Then, in 1928, came the move to Seventh and C streets, where Hamilton's reached its zenith in architectural elegance and grocery excellence which made its employees proud to claim, "I work at Hamilton's."

What a rise from a plain Victorian store to Hamilton's of silvered columns, silvered lettering, velvet drapes, two floors and a mezzanine, a basement, 70 employees and a fleet of red van-type delivery trucks engraved with "Hamilton's" in gold letters!

In the basement was the telephone order department, where telephone girls took orders from every section of the county. The orders would be filled upstairs and then routed to the red delivery trucks, which were usually on time.

The 35-seat soda fountain which occupied the west side of the store was so popular that you had to stand behind a stool and wait for a diner to finish before you could get one of those wonderful milk shakes and a prize salad. Folks who worked downtown raced at noon to mount the fountain seats first.

Townsfolk remember Hamilton as a gray-bearded, gray-haired, distinguished man, dressed in a neat gray suit, white shirt and tie, spending some time at his favorite place, the coffee counter, where he would grind beans and sack the grounds and chat with customers just as he did when he first started his grocery business.

He was spoken of as the most honest man in town. For instance, he advertised eggs from the Poway Valley one summer as being "as fresh as could be expected in midsummer," eggs other merchants would have called strictly farm-fresh.

He died in 1933, five years after his new store was dedicated, and his son, Thomas Hamilton, took over as company president. Hamilton's later was sold to the Leighton's cafeteria firm and eventually closed.

Now great chain-store supermarkets duplicate themselves in sprawling centers throughout the county, and downtown is overshadowed by high-rise office buildings.

But who can forget Hamilton's own plum pudding, dipped in a special glaze, Hamilton's own brandy sauce, 42 different Hamilton-baked bread items, Hamilton's Christmas boxes of dried fruit and nuts from all over the world, cookies from England, dates from the Mideast, litchi nuts from China, coffee from Brazil and decorated cakes for all occasions? Some still believe they can savor in memory the Elysian fragrances that wafted from Hamilton's bakery and candy departments, and the taste buds still drool. That was the wonderful store of Charles S. Hamilton.

MARSTON'S

For almost 50 years, Marston's department store at the northeast corner of Fifth Avenue and C Street was the center of the action, the color, the warmth and the beauty of the Christmas shopping season in San Diego.

"Let me off at Marston's, please," was a familiar request to street-car motormen from shoppers coming down Fifth. People dressed to go downtown, as they dressed for church on Sunday, the women with hats and gloves.

Customers bought from Marston's generation after generation, for it stood on its comfortable old location from 1912 to 1961, when Marston's sold out to the Broadway Hale chain. The building was finally torn down in 1969 to make way for a modern structure.

Downtown is no longer a major retail center, and the department store business has mostly moved out to huge, anonymous, chain-dominated shopping centers in the suburbs.

But Marston's had a long run and was remarkably stable and predictable while it lasted. One matron recalled that she bought shoes for her wedding from the same salesman who had sold her shoes as a child.

The toy department was in the basement and some of the mothers took advantage of Marston's patience and stamina by leaving their children to visit a jolly Santa Claus and to browse among the toys while they shopped upstairs.

Customers found high quality, the very best, at Marston's. A Marston label was a badge of quality.

Often downtown you would hear, "I'll meet you at Marston's." That meant the C Street entrance, under the marquee, where the elegantly uniformed door captain, Charles Walker, graciously greeted so many customers for so many years—from rich dowagers in long black limousines to housewives driving up in flivvers. A person felt thoroughly metropolitan, sophisticated and welcome after being ushered into the store by Charley.

"Charley was a very fine man," Hamilton Marston remembers. Hamilton is the grandson of the late George White Marston, the store founder.

The Christmas shoppers at Marston's found good scents, neat and courteous clerks all in their places, good spirits, pleasant vibrations and exquisite floral decorations. They found a kind of nobility without condescension, crisp efficiency without surliness and dignity without stuffiness.

The customers walked in wide aisles, and much of the merchandise was in shiny glass display cases. They were impressed by the dignified, patient, immaculately dressed floorwalkers with boutonnieres like Frederick Chasey, a Britisher who reigned on the first floor.

In the early days the store was bustling with boys running cash payments and credit slips to the cashiers. Then came the cash baskets rattling overhead on trolleys. Then came whooshing pneumatic tubes. Your change returned in a tube with a bang.

Great attention was given to the large street display windows. And the interior of the store was decorated with massive floral displays—poinsettias at Christmas time from the Paul Ecke ranch at Encinitas, lilacs at Easter from the Franklin Barnes ranch at Julian.

The customers might notice a handsome, white-haired, elderly, neatly dressed gentleman calling the employees on all floors by their names as he walked through the store. That was George White Marston, the founder.

He came to San Diego, population 1,500, in 1870, clerked at the Horton House (where the U.S. Grant Hotel now stands), worked in two general stores, bought one of them in partnership with Charles S. Hamilton in 1872, and five years later opened his own dry goods store. Indians used to sit on the ledge outside his store, giving it a frontier atmosphere. He moved three times to different locations downtown before the store arrived at its final site.

He died in 1946, leaving an amazing record of civic accomplishments and contributions. He was one of San Diego's all-time best men, and he not only gave to this city a wonderful store, a store with a heart, but he left an example of vision, initiative, business acumen, honesty, generosity, courtesy and compassion.

SOUTH MISSION BEACH

Believe it or not, there was a time in San Diego when folks scoffed at the idea of living year round at the beach.

"Why, that's just a place to change your bathing suit!" was the common comment.

In the 1930s, the discoverers came—the people who wanted permanent residences at South Mission Beach, especially. The newcomers found a paradise of fun, sun and health.

The population of South Mission Beach consisted of judges, doctors, newsmen, attorneys, teachers, retirees and just plain folks. Young and old enjoyed that stretch of bay shore and seashore, unmarred by crime.

They found to their pleasant surprise that property lots sold for a low price—one inside lot went for $332.50 when sold by the Mission Beach Co. It was a sand lot, 30 feet by 80 feet, crowned with verbena. Upon that lot the buyer put up a house of two bedrooms, a bath, garage and fireplace. Later, another room and bath were added. It was only about 100 feet from the bay. Jutting into the bay from the bayfront homes were picturesque piers, from which the residents fished, dived and speared fish.

Mullet were plentiful in the bay waters. Men ranged the shore gathering clams and squid. Gulls cried in the sky and lumbering pelicans scudded overhead. It was an aquatic dreamland.

The big and world-famous Mission Bay Park didn't come into existence until the 1950s. Before it was dredged out to create blue water and man-made beaches of sparkling sand, some detractors of Mission Bay sneered at the expanse as a "swamp." It was an area of great marshes, sloughs, grasses, and a swift channel current running beneath the Ocean Beach bridge to the surf and sea beyond.

To the boys of Mission Beach years ago, it was a wonderland of fishing, boating, swimming, bait hunting, spearing, sailing. It was their own realm of quiet air, of beach and gulls and sunning, of fish and birds, wooden piers ingrained with the scent of the sea—a place where Mother Nature could safely roam, and so could a boy.

On weekends, old Mission Bay often took on a bustling holiday air, when her smoother waters were furrowed by charging boats and rumpled by swimmers, and her natural calm was disturbed by shouts and calls. Fishermen tried their luck on the channel and up the sloughs, and contesting sails skimmed in sometimes close array.

Then it was Monday along the shore. The visitors were gone and their foreign noises had faded away. The cleansing tide flushed the bay clean of picnic flotsam and litter. The whole scene was blessed by peaceful quiet. The democracy of wildlife could convene once more before the entranced eyes of a boy.

In early morning, Mrs. Mallard formed her little flotilla of ducklings into line and launched them for their breakfast, all the while admonishing them to stay near. Other birds rose busily from their marsh retreats and clucked and chirped the reveille of another beautiful day. A dignified white egret stood tall and erect in the water surveying his domain. An echelon of speeding teal winged over. A mullet leaped from the water and then fell back, buried in ripples. A pair of noisy and embattled Western sea gulls wrangled and tugged at a coveted morsel, abandoned in the sand by a picknicker. While they were fighting, a sea gull hijacker swooped down upon them, pirated the morsel for himself and quickly made his getaway.

A morning sun tinted the water with glory.

A helldiver, like a feathered punt, bobbed along the surface and then suddenly disappeared, scattering panicked minnows. Snipes skittered over a bleached stretch of beach in a long-beaked revue, forever hunting and forever poking in anxious harvest of mysterious bits of food. Cute little sandpipers, called sanderlings or peeps, kept them company in stiff-legged rhythm.

It was a morning of exquisite peace, when those who knew the bay loved it best.

Men with foreign faces walked the shallows looking for bait and squid. Clams for fish bait were another fringe benefit of living in those quiet days along the shores of Mission Bay.

The shadows of kelp bass were seen in the grass not far from shore by a lonely fisherman with his poles and bait boxes, staking out his place on the bay sand, baiting his hooks with hope and small fillets from razor clams dug along the shore.

On the bridge down the bay, old men with long bamboo poles started angling for smelt that would be used later for bait in quest of halibut.

There came a time when the inhabitants of the stretch of bay beach began to call themselves the happy people of South Mission Beach. Every now and then, they would get out their big cook pots and stage a fish stew feast on the sand. The delicious ingredients—fish, clams, crabs and more—came from the bay. The big event was the Sunday morning volleyball game played on the sand. And then the players dived into the cool waters of the bay. The folks of Mission Beach virtually lived in their bathing suits, shorts, halters and bare skin. There was ping-pong, sailing, rowing and other diversion. Sometimes, for a change of pace, people would go to the amusement center and ride the roller coaster.

All of this, and much more, helps to explain why the residents of old South Mission Beach were such a happy and loving group.

MAX MILLER

The waterfront once was a quaint, salty, fishy, wind-battered, fascinating little realm of boats, birds, fishermen, sailors, tourists, characters, shoreboats and raw natural beauty.

It is all in the book, *I Cover the Waterfront*, written in 1932 by a San Diego newspaper's waterfront reporter, Max Miller. Rereading that book revives nostalgia for days when the water was clearer, the liners came in at night with lights shining, booted fishermen were abroad in San Diego Bay, and there was peace and color and charm in the more natural shoreline.

It's a little late to be reviewing the book, but the waterfront is a locus of attention as preparations go forward for the America's Cup races here. Over the decades, new construction has altered the quality of life along the waterfront and more changes may be expected in the offing.

Miller's book is still in the libraries and now and then the past surfaces at the shore. The pelicans and sea gulls remind us that they are still around. Some bamboo-pole fishermen still squat on piers. Shore boats come in.

Max has gone. His battered desk at the old tugboat office upstairs is gone. So are the pictures of barracuda and mackerel and other fish that used to decorate the press room walls. Sea gulls used to look in the window at him and one time he wrote: "I have been here so long that even the sea gulls must recognize me. They must pass the word from generation to generation, from egg to egg."

Every now and then, and sometimes at night, a passenger liner from the East Coast would make a call at San Diego. The waterfront reporters, including Miller, would go out in a shore boat to meet the liner before she docked in the harbor, and after the quarantine flag had been lowered. The reporters enjoyed good food and liquor aboard and shook the hands of celebrities like Jack Dempsey, Charlie Chaplin and Babe Ruth.

Max might be dismayed if he were to cover the waterfront today. He would find no saltwater-soaked, artistic, wind-worn little wooden piers where old skiffs were tied. And would today's gulls look in a window at him?

Tuna fishermen are an endangered species. The sardines, which once buried the decks of boats hip-deep in a silver flood, disappeared and the waterfront canneries have all closed down.

Max became famous. All the saltwater, seaside material in his book fascinated the folks from the dusty Plains and the echoing concrete canyons of the East. The movies bought the title of the book and Max wrote for Hollywood for a spell. A song was written called "I Cover the Waterfront."

But Max wasn't spoiled by fame. He was a serious environmentalist and deplored the greed and the growth. He was critical of certain agencies he charged were helping to cause pollution and overpopulation.

He had one explanation for growth in San Diego. "It has become overcrowded," he wrote, "because tourists do not long remain tourists. Next time they return, they bring all their folks to stay."

SAN DIEGO BAY

Many visitors from Cornland and Wheatland took one look at San Diego Bay and declared:

"This is the place." And then they moved here.

The first attraction they might have seen was the sea gull, which was here when the Spanish explorers, led by the Portuguese navigator Juan Rodriguez Cabrillo, first looked on the bay in 1542, only 50 years after the first voyage of Christopher Columbus.

Then came the Mexicans and the Yankees. Again the gulls turned out to greet them. Whenever history was made in San Diego, the gulls were watching.

If this city ever suffers a nuclear holocaust, the sea gull again will be there, mewing a lonely dirge over the charred ruins.

The long-running Sea Gull Follies shows the voracious seabirds coming and going, swooping and swirling, kak-kak calling and battling each other for food. They're flying goats. They'll eat almost anything that floats—potato chips, picnic leavings, the eggs of other birds, slices of bread thrown into the air, garbage, old fish, bait and an incredible variety of outrageous refuse. They are the gleaners and cleaners of shore and shallows, first in line in the "Keep Our Beaches Clean" brigade.

Clouds of the clamorous birds used to follow the old garbage scows as they slowly chug-chugged out of the bay to their dumping place at sea.

Strangers to an earlier San Diego Bay used to marvel at the sight of giant log rafts being towed into the harbor on long hawsers. They had come by sea from the Columbia River. The house of a gawking newcomer often was built with boards sawn here at the waterfront that still had about them the aroma of the sea.

There was a bonus for waterfront watchers in the early 1930s, when a lone old sailing ship from the War of 1812 was towed into port and berthed here. It was "Old Ironsides," the famous wooden *USS Constitution*, built in 1797 and memorialized in Oliver Wendell Holmes' poem beginning, "Aye, tear her tattered ensign down, long has it waved on high." The ship was towed back to Boston, where it is still berthed.

Tourists on the waterfront poked their noses into bait houses near the ferry terminal to examine the emporiums of clams, crawfish, worms and sardines.

If the bay watchers had been here in the last century, they would have seen colorful and picturesque Chinese junks swaying and bobbing in the bay. The Chinese were our first commercial fishermen. They taught the Yankees to like abalone.

And if the lookie-loos had been around in 1908, they would have had a close-up view of President Teddy Roosevelt's Great White Fleet, an armada of 16 battleships, seven destroyers and four auxiliaries. The bay water was not deep enough for the battle wagons, so they moored in Coronado Roads, in the ocean outside the port, and sailors came ashore in boats.

There was a hot time in the old town when those sailors came ashore. The lights blinked merrily for the boys in blue in the Stingaree district south of Broadway, the city's naughty area.

Tuna fishermen mended and dried their nets along the bay's Embarcadero to the delight of strollers.

Some old boys remember with smiles the good old days when they could skinny-dip in the bay without fear of arrest—until, perhaps, John Law came around on horseback.

There were bathhouses in the shallows of the bay. Kyle's, at the foot of Fifth, was one of the most popular of the plunges.

Young men sculled in the bay with swift, powerful strokes. They shoved off from the San Diego Rowing Club, which occupied a site on the bay for many years before moving to Mission Bay. The old boathouse is now a waterfront restaurant.

Almost forgotten are the bum boats, small craft that plied among the bay's water traffic, peddling a variety of commodities to large vessels.

On the older bay was the fireboat Bill Kettner. What a grand sight it was to see the Kettner with its hoses going full blast!

World War II drew a tight security curtain around the bay. No more civilian watchers could sit with binoculars looking for seals and seabirds.

The curtain wasn't lifted until the war was won. And then things seemed to have changed. The old bay was gone.

WORLD WAR II

During World War II, the city became an arsenal of war. It was a restless, noisy, hectic, hurry-up scene of a city crowded with servicemen and women, defense workers, bobby-soxers, townspeople, profiteers and criminals, a strange mingling of patriotism and greed.

Horton Plaza throbbed with people coming and going, shouting hello and goodbye, and climbing aboard streetcars and buses. Lunch pails were as numerous as the defense workers who carried them. It was a saluting war downtown: fuzzy-chinned GIs were energetic in hand-waving at the brass.

You couldn't get near strategic places on the waterfront. Barrage balloons could be seen in the sky up beyond downtown. A sea of white hats moved up Broadway. Barkers stood outside their stands trying to lure GIs and sailors inside. Great blasts of noise belched from saloons when the doors were opened.

The city was jammed. Authorities, both local and national, asked that travelers not visit San Diego or any other defense town unless they were vital to the war effort. There was to be no tourism for the duration. A sign advised: "Ration travel. Save the seats for the boys." Posters everywhere appealed: "Buy war bonds and stamps."

The population of San Diego boomed, increasing more than 40 percent in four wartime years.

For the first time, women wore pants downtown. Never before had the city seen a female city trash truck driver, a female cabdriver, a female barber, freight loader, or filling station attendant. There was even a female Santa Claus. A sign in a defense plant advertised for women security guards "to release men security guards for combat war duty." At some tavern doors, women stood guard and examined the IDs of servicemen to see that the under-age recruits and boots were not sneaking in.

The favorite hair-do for women was the pompadour and curled bangs, often worn with a snood to keep long hair out of the machinery in defense plants. Women defense workers walked in the middle of dark side streets at night, to thwart the mashers who swept in with the tide of humanity.

Bars sprouted. The bars went dark at midnight,

and the cops were thankful for that. Downtown was well policed by both local officers and military police. Before closing time, downtown was one big jukebox lighted up and blaring out. The songs were "Small Hotel," "I'll Be Seeing You," "Long Ago and Far Away" and various anthems of the state of Texas.

A sign in a store proclaimed, "Texas Spoken Here." People brought their own shopping bags to carry purchases home, because of the paper shortage. Cars parked on downtown streets showed the signs of long wear. There were no new cars for civilians. The queues at some places downtown got so long that people took to bringing folding chairs. There was a run on stores selling maps, globes and atlases, as people sought to pinpoint the fighting fronts.

There was a Ferris wheel operating near Fourth and E. A number of mysterious small gray structures were scattered around downtown. They were military prophylactic stations. Washington had shut down all red-light houses to protect the GIs and war workers from venereal diseases. But the "Sea Gulls," the girls who followed the fleet, came in greater numbers. Servicemen on Broadway walked by the carnies trying to separate the military pay dollars from young GIs by offering hot dogs, Texas turtles, love potions, knives, cheap watches, illicit booze, filthy pictures, good-luck charms, pennants, souvenirs and hundred of other bits of war-town merchandise. At an arcade, a young boot could get peanuts out of a machine, gaze at mechanical peep shows, test his punching power on a gadget and play some marble games.

Tijuana's downtown also was jumping. Americanos searched for meat, butter, sugar, shoes, silk stockings, tires, gasoline, perfume—all the luxuries wartime rationing had made scarce or impossible to find in San Diego.

And then came the day when The Tribune-Sun's Page One banner screamed in red ink, "NAZIS QUIT!" Lee B. Cusick, San Diego's wartime manpower director, appealed to defense workers to stay on the job. There was still Japan to defeat.

San Diego still had some war memories to collect before that moment came.

But the cry of a sea gull overhead seemed to offer the promise of eventual peace in a war-weary world.

HOUSING IN WAR TOWN

The war on the home front brought out the worst and best in the humans participating, especially in the housing market, where greed came up against patriotism.

Hapless defense workers, military wives, job seekers, officials and crooks trudged the streets in the second gold rush, looking for housing. Housing hunters crowded restaurants, all-night theaters, USO centers, the Y's and other Community Chest agencies, Red Cross offices, churches, depots, hotels and streets.

It was a restless time. Millions of migrant workers were on the move, many from farms. Military units were shuttled from area to area.

Chambers of Commerce in defense-bulging cities put out reverse propaganda: "Don't come until after the war. Stay away unless you are being recruited for war work. Our city is crowded. Buy war bonds!"

No Vacancy signs were everywhere, and still they came, looking for a place to stay. Newspaper classified ads pleaded: "Ill baby and mother need place to stay," "Wounded veteran must have room," "Army veteran's wife needs housing." A USO worker made 50 calls before locating a room for two Navy wives. Newspaper obituary columns were scanned closely for leads to housing.

Many patriotic widows in San Diego, some of them Gold Star mothers, opened their homes to stranded defense workers. But some landlords were hostile to people from different parts of the country speaking with different accents, to families with children and to non-whites. Those prejudices were keenly resented.

Tents, hallways, trailer camps, converted garages and barns, tar-paper shacks, basements, attics, lean-tos and streetcars were used as shelter.

Workers shared hotel rooms with a half-dozen snoring men. Couples alternated using beds in a room they rented jointly. Those working the night shift used the room and bed during the day, while the day-shift workers slept there at night. What they did on their days off was a mystery.

The war cities never slept. Some beds were never cold.

The crisis was even felt in the police press room at the foot of Market Street, a place reserved for newspapermen. A police reporter who had the early shift unlocked the door to the sacrosanct place and was struck by the unmistakable, alien fragrance of perfume. Scattered on the floor and on typewriters and desks was an array of frilly and lacy things. Two girls lay stretched out on the couch covered by rough jail blankets tucked under their chins. Stranded in San Diego and unable to find a room, they had appealed to the desk lieutenant for housing and he had presumptuously assigned them to the press room.

It took two days for the feminine scents to dissipate and be replaced with the familiar old fragrances of bourbon, tobacco smoke and shoe polish.

THE BLACK MARKET

The people gave blood until they were groggy. They slaved 10 hours a day in factories. They bought bonds until they were broke. They shared their homes, their cars, their garages, their tools, even their precious booze. They served the defense effort day and night. They went with holes in their shoes and knotted shoelaces. They went short on toilet paper. The women went without silk stockings, bare-legged.

But they shopped in the illegal black market. Most of the home-fronters were loyal and patriotic, but they were also loyal to their stomachs. Many reverted to the sneaky ways of Prohibition. They side-mouthed their requests for black-market food and for black-market liquor, clothes, gas and cigarettes, as they had done in the 1920s at the door grills of speakeasies.

Sociologists explained that the black market flourished because Americans always disobey laws they don't like. People had high wages and full employment for the first time in years and they yearned for a departure from the frugal, just-past Depression, a time when they had no money, no jobs, no hope and enjoyed very little in the midst of plenty of food and goods. The defense workers' wallets were fat with money, their pockets heavy with change. Some defense workers didn't even bother to pick up pennies or nickels when they dropped them.

People were going to get theirs even if they had to steal it. Burglars prowling homes stole food stamps and gas coupons first, money and jewelry later. Counterfeiters, some in tiny wildcat print shops, copied the stamps and coupons and peddled the phonies on the black market.

Some people who had never before been seduced by wrongdoing grinned evilly and passed the bogus tender. They consorted as customers with hoodlums. They spent outrageous sums for hard-to-get, under-the-counter commodities and visited creepy joints in sleazy neighborhoods to get them. Many civic saints winked at their consciences. They rationalized that they couldn't fight the war on the home front on a diet of vegetable steaks, sauerkraut and pig's knuckles or beefless stew, of which there seemed to be plenty.

Unfortunately, there was no black market for a segment of the home-front population who sorely needed dry goods—babies. Millions of them were caught with their diapers down. There are millions of people in America today who do not know the agony endured by their fathers to find them diapers, bottles, nipples and safety pins.

There was nothing, absolutely nothing, to top the ecstasy and exultation of the discovery and purchase of an acutely short item. It buoyed the war-torn psyche and gave a civilian—especially if he were a 4-F—more confidence and self-esteem. It cheered the women at home, drew respect from the children and filled the deep pockets of black commerce with gold.

Many government price-control officials, plus many volunteers, were arrayed against the black market, the hoarders and the cheaters, but the dark commerce thrived anyhow. Some fat-fingered knaves emerged from the war years heavy with loot. It was even suspected that they were sorry when peace was proclaimed.

CORONADO FERRY

It was a sad night on Aug. 3, 1969, when the ferry boats that had plied between San Diego and Coronado for more than 80 years made their last run, and the new bay bridge went into service.

What a thrill it was for the boys and girls of yesterday to plow across the bay, especially in the fog or rain, to the accompaniment of the creakings and groanings of the vessel, the slap of the water against the hull, the churning of the wheel, the moaning fog horns, the bells ringing, the swish of the wake and the cry of gulls overhead!

When you bought your tickets at the ferry ticket office, at the foot of Market Street and a short distance from the slips, you caught the smell of tar from the slips, which were V's of hefty log pilings where the ferries would nose in at the end of a run.

It was only a 10-minute ride across the bay, but to the kids it was a real voyage. The ferries left every 20 minutes, so there was never a long wait. Once aboard, the small fry would scramble to the top deck to watch the foamy water drip from the sloshing old paddle wheels.

The five ferries bought by the state and retired from service at midnight of the day the bridge was opened to traffic were all driven by propellers, but sidewheelers had been the rule for many years.

The ferry names were on everybody's tongue—the *Crown City, San Diego, Silver Strand, Morena, Ramona, Silver Gate* and *Benicia.*

Now there are rumors that, when the bridge bonds are paid off, the ferries may come back. The first in line for tickets, no doubt, will be the old captains, engineers and deckhands.

With their lights sparkling in the darkness and reflected upon the bay at night, the ferries were beautiful when viewed from shore. From the decks, passengers enjoyed picture post-card views of San Diego and Coronado. And to their worshipers, the squat little ferries were beautiful, going and coming and moored, morning, noon and night.

WHY PEOPLE CAME

As San Diego geared up the rosy rhetoric for the America's Cup races, brought the Super Bowl here and sought business for a new convention center, the language of self-praise used in the past to entice people and capital to our soil returned to memory.

We were "Eden by the sea, this paradise, this sun-splashed haven, this heaven on earth."

Explorer Juan Rodriguez Cabrillo, the first European to see San Diego Bay, had some nice things to say about it, and there followed through the centuries a procession of amateur and professional boosters extolling the virtues of this lovely land in books, brochures, letters, magazines and posters and by word of mouth.

Even the bright labels on California fruit crates, depicting wonderful oranges, lemons, apricots and other bounty, were part of the propaganda.

Great events helped, such as the visit of the Great White Fleet here in 1908, when thousands of sailors first tasted the sweets of our town. Many of them returned later to become residents. And both world wars brought many servicemen here for training and they returned with their families in peacetime.

More drawing power was added by the two magnificent expositions held in Balboa Park in 1915-16 and 1935-36.

The annual Rose Bowl classic at Pasadena, showing the rest of the country palm trees, blue skies, women in shorts and men without coats, no doubt has turned many a Midwestern or Eastern family toward California as a permanent residence.

Here was opportunity, climate, health, romance and freedom—as advertised in the lyrics of songs like "California, Here I Come" and more recently "California Dreamin'."

In the 1920s on a cold blustery day, a Midwesterner received a letter from a San Diego friend. The recipient did not miss the engraving of a warm sun and green orange grove in a corner of the envelope. The letter said, in part:

"Nature has been generous with San Diego. This is truly heaven on earth, and each year I like it better. I have only spent a few dollars so far this winter for fuel, which is kerosene. We use it in oil stoves. Furnaces are scarce here. The children are tan and healthy. They get all the fresh fruit they want. My wife is very happy here. The bays and the ocean are beautiful and blue. Everybody expects business to grow. There is great opportunity for you here. Maybe I sound like a professional California booster, but I sometimes believe this wonderful place is what nature intended as a paradise. This is the best of our country. Come out and live, man." He did.

In January 1870, the San Diego Chamber of Commerce was organized "to take some practical steps to unite the businessmen of the city for the better promotion of the public interests." It had a marvelous product to sell. "San Diego is the natural commercial center of a vast scope of country, rich in mineral and agricultural wealth, embracing all of Southern California, southern Nevada, Arizona, New Mexico and northern Mexico," one of the chamber's first brochures proclaims. Brave words for a tiny town.

The San Diego California Club, said to have been the first booster organization of its kind in the nation, was formed in 1919, with Oscar W. Cotton as its secretary. A typical advertisement of the club said, in part: "Plenty of room at reasonable rates. Almost too good to be true. But it is more than true. Modern and spacious quarters are available, at moderate rentals, in the hotels at San Diego, Southern California's beautiful seaside city."

The ad promised visitors "wonderfully alluring beauties and attractions that make each day a bewilderment of happiness."

But nobody had to drive east on Interstate 8 at 5 p.m. in those days.

Gov. Edmund G. Brown announced proudly in 1963 that California was the most populated state in the union, having passed New York state to become No. 1. The Golden State reveled in its bigness and importance. But even then there were those who glumly remarked that some day Californians would rue their population supremacy, instead of celebrating it.

WILD FLOWERS THAT WERE

The hills of California once were green, brown, golden, blue and white, and there were no natural gardens in the world which were so big, so rich or so beautiful. Mother Nature used a lavish brush in coloring the mesas, the valleys, the streamsides and the foothills of the Golden State with such magnificent wildflowers.

The curtain would rise on her spring display across the state, and that included San Diego County. What a time for the bees!

There are—or have been—some 6,000 different flowering plants in California, some drab but important for grazing, others pure delight to the eye of the settler and the traveler weary of the somber grays and browns of winter.

It takes a botanist to identify many of the various blooms but Mr. Ordinary can match the scientist in appreciation of the flowers.

Mustard—green and yellow—may be a plebeian weed, but its petals and stems splash the fields with noble color. In older Mission Beach, when there were still large vacant lots here and there, wild buttercups yellowed the sand lots. And the sand verbena added its beauty.

San Diegans who enjoyed the wildflowers when the town was younger and more natural remember the delicate and fragrant shooting star. Along Reynard Way and on the sides of canyons running into that street, the purplish stars in their proud and pretty patches competed with the blue lupine and mustard, the figwort and violets for the glory of spring.

What former San Diego boy has not sprawled in a bed of shooting stars and lupine and gazed at fluffy white clouds against an azure sky without dreaming of glory and gold? The springtime is the time for rosy dreams.

While back-weary home gardeners tried to coax blooms from their reluctant flower beds, the wild-flowers in early times thrived all by themselves with nature.

In really old days, a star performer in the ranks of wildflowers was the yerba buena, the good herb, of delicate fragrance. Its slender stems trailing on the ground bloomed with small white and purplish flowers. The plant was used by the Indians and early settlers as a tea and as a medicine for fevers and stomach complaints.

Kate Sessions, San Diego's famous horticulturist, introduced wild bluish lilac to her yard after finding it growing wild in the back country. The California lilac inhabits brushy places from one end of California to the other. In the more remote parts of our back country, you can still see them brightening up the brush with colors shading from deep blue to lavender, light blue and white.

Another flower our California dreaming boy found in his favorite canyon in San Diego was the lupine. It is not finicky about where it takes root, is blue and may be annual, perennial or even woody. It is a hardy flower, coming up today bright in some unlikely places, like vacant lots, alongside roads and on bare hills.

The California poppy is one of the first heralds of spring. Once it glowed in great sheets of color and was framed against the lush green grass in meadows and on hillsides. Glossy yellow and deep orange, it is the official state flower of California. Poppies were widespread, thick and so bright that flaming foothills once served as beacons to ships at sea. Now the poppy is sadly in decline, in San Diego and the rest of California.

The majestic Spanish bayonet, pride of the yucca family, rises on the chaparral hillsides of San Diego County like handsome soldiers at attention. The white to purplish blossoms, tall stalks and stiff, swordlike leaves present an impressive array, particularly in the Borrego Valley. They are protected by law and no longer can motorists leave the desert with bayonets tied to the running boards.

Many wildflowers are becoming rare, but they have their friends, such as the California Native Plant Society, and a wildflower sanctuary has been set aside in the Antelope Valley. Many people, on their own, scatter seeds in good growing places to help perpetuate one of California's greatest assets, its lovely flowers growing wild.

Those who arrived before so many colorful hills were plowed under can count themselves fortunate to have seen the breathtaking sight of whole hillsides painted gold and blue with thousands upon thousands of poppies and lupines.

THE LITTLE PADRE

It was raining when I reached the Carmel mission and somehow the beat of the falling drops, the wind and the grayness outside emphasized the ascetic character of the plain little room in the Mission San Carlos Borromeo del Rio Carmel. Here in this cell Father Junipero Serra died on Aug. 28, 1784, at the age of 70.

He founded the Mission San Diego de Alcala, the first European settlement on the Pacific Coast of what is now America and the first of nine missions founded by the little Franciscan friar.

While Serra was founding two of his missions—San Francisco and San Juan Capistrano—in 1776, American colonists across the continent were loosening the bonds with England, killing the redcoats and declaring their independence from the rule of George III.

The mission in the beautiful Carmel valley is described as the most beautiful of California missions. It is on a hillside overlooking a fertile plain. Serra made it his headquarters as father-president of the entire chain.

He walked great distances past the lupine and poppies of El Camino Real, visiting his missions, even though he was never robust. While walking in 1740 from Vera Cruz to Mexico City, he was bitten by an insect. Infection set in, and he suffered a painful lameness for the rest of his life.

Serra's devotion to his work was said to have been an inspiration to those who followed in his footsteps. The visitor wondered if in his last moments, Serra returned in memory to July 16, 1769, when he dedicated his first mission in San Diego, which he always called the mother mission.

That was the beginning of our town, now a great city, bursting with wealth and energy, crowded with people who are dedicated to personal goals like ambition, pleasure and happiness and who seldom give much thought to the nobility of asceticism and self-sacrifice.

The night before he died, he spent most of his time on his knees in prayer on the bare, cold floor of his simple room, despite his lame leg, congested lungs and a high fever. Earlier in the day before his death, he had walked 100 yards to the original wooden church for Mass and then returned to the room where he died.

Death came to him quietly. Clad in the simple friar's robe in which he died, Serra was placed in a coffin with six candles burning beside it. Indian neophytes wept. The mission bells tolled his passing. Knowing death was near, the little friar had asked the mission carpenter to make him a plain wooden coffin.

He was a small man, 5 feet 2 or 3 inches tall, but his frail body contained a determination, a stubbornness, a purpose and a ferocity that emerged when the welfare of his missions, his friars and his Indian neophytes was at issue. His room was simple and frugal but his achievements were grand and glorious.

If he could return today, Serra no doubt would be proud to view the 21 restored missions, so replete with mementos of his labors and those of his fellows. But he would fret over the disappearance of the Indians from the missions.

Now he is a candidate for sainthood and his life is being studied by scholars in the Vatican. And when the mission bells ring today in the Mission San Diego, they seem to toll joyously for the devout little cowled friar who prayed as he limped from mission to mission, or rode his little donkey in Old California.